Piano/Vocal

THE WORLD'S GREAT CLASSICAL MUSIC

Gilbert and Sullivan

67 Selections from 13 Operettas

EDITED BY RICHARD WALTERS
JOSEPH HENRY, ASSISTANT EDITOR

ISBN 0-634-02754-9

HAL•LEONARD®
CORPORATION

7777 W. BLUEMOUND RD. P.O. BOX 13819 MILWAUKEE, WI 53213

Visit Hal Leonard Online at
www.halleonard.com

CONTENTS

TRIAL BY JURY

17   When First My Old, Old Love I Knew

20   Oh, Gentlemen, Listen, I Pray

THE SORCERER

23   Time Was, When Love and I

27   Happy Young Heart

31   My Name Is John Wellington Wells

H.M.S. PINAFORE

40   We Sail the Ocean Blue

44   I'm Called Little Buttercup

48   A Maiden Fair to See

51   I Am the Captain of the *Pinafore*

55   Sorry Her Lot Who Loves Too Well

59   I Am the Monarch of the Sea

62   When I Was a Lad I

66   Refrain, Audacious Tar

72   Fair Moon, to Thee I Sing

76   A Simple Sailor Lowly Born

84   He Is an Englishman!

THE PIRATES OF PENZANCE

87   When Frederic Was a Little Lad

90   I Am a Pirate King

94   Oh, Is There Not One Maiden Breast

98   Poor Wand'ring One

105   I Am the Very Model of a Modern Major-General

114   The Policeman's Song

117   With Cat-Like Tread, Upon Our Prey We Steal

PATIENCE

124   Twenty Love-Sick Maidens We

132   When I First Put This Uniform On

135   Am I Alone and Unobserved?

142   Prithee, Pretty Maiden

144   Silver'd Is the Women's Hair

149   Love Is a Plaintive Song

IOLANTHE

152   The Law Is the True Embodiment

155   When I Went to the Bar as a Very Young Man

158   When All Night Long a Chap Remains

162   When Britain Really Ruled the Waves

164   Oh, Foolish Fay

167   Love, Unrequited, Robs Me of My Rest

PRINCESS IDA

179   If You Give Me Your Attention

182   Oh, Goddess Wise

THE MIKADO

185   A Wand'ring Minstrel I

194   As Some Day It May Happen

199   Three Little Maids from School Are We

205   The Sun, Whose Rays Are All Ablaze

208   Miya-Sama

214   The Mikado's Song

221   The Flowers That Bloom in the Spring

226   Alone, and Yet Alive

230   Willow, Tit-Willow

232   There Is Beauty in the Bellow of the Blast

RUDDIGORE

237   If Somebody There Chanced to Be

241   My Boy, You May Take It From Me

244   To a Garden Full of Posies

246   Henceforth All the Crimes

THE YEOMAN OF THE GUARD

250   When Maiden Loves, She Sits and Sighs

253   Is Life a Boon?

257   I Have a Song to Sing, O!

267   I've Jibe and Joke

271   Were I Thy Bride

277   Oh! A Private Buffoon Is a Light-Hearted Loon

281   Free from His Fetters Grim

THE GONDOLIERS

284   The Duke of Plaza-Toro

287   No Possible Doubt Whatever

291   When a Merry Maiden Marries

297   Rising Early in the Morning

304   Take a Pair of Sparkling Eyes

308   There Lived a King

317   On the Day When I Was Wedded

UTOPIA LIMITED

322   In Ev'ry Mental Lore

THE GRAND DUKE

328   So Ends My Dream

Alphabetically by Song

226   Alone, and Yet Alive (The Mikado)

135   Am I Alone and Unobserved? (Patience)

194   As Some Day It May Happen (The Mikado)

284   The Duke of Plaza-Toro (The Gondoliers)

72   Fair Moon, to Thee I Sing (H.M.S. Pinafore)

221   The Flowers That Bloom in the Spring (The Mikado)

281   Free from His Fetters Grim (The Yeoman of the Guard)

27   Happy Young Heart (The Sorcerer)

84   He Is an Englishman! (H.M.S. Pinafore)

246   Henceforth All the Crimes (Ruddigore)

90   I Am a Pirate King (The Pirates of Penzance)

51   I Am the Captain of the Pinafore (H.M.S. Pinafore)

59   I Am the Monarch of the Sea (H.M.S. Pinafore)

105   I Am the Very Model of a Modern Major-General (The Pirates of Penzance)

257   I Have a Song to Sing, O! (The Yeoman of the Guard)

44   I'm Called Little Buttercup (H.M.S. Pinafore)

267   I've Jibe and Joke (The Yeoman of the Guard)

237   If Somebody There Chanced to Be (Ruddigore)

179   If You Give Me Your Attention (Princess Ida)

322   In Ev'ry Mental Lore (Utopia Limited)

253   Is Life a Boon? (The Yeoman of the Guard)

152   The Law Is the True Embodiment (Iolanthe)

149   Love Is a Plaintive Song (Patience)

167   Love, Unrequited, Robs Me of My Rest (Iolanthe)

48   A Maiden Fair to See (H.M.S. Pinafore)

214   The Mikado's Song (The Mikado)

208   Miya Sama (The Mikado)

241   My Boy, You May Take It from Me (Ruddigore)

31   My Name Is John Wellington Wells (The Sorcerer)

287   No Possible Doubt Whatever (The Gondoliers)

277   Oh! A Private Buffoon Is a Light-Hearted Loon (The Yeoman of the Guard)

164   Oh, Foolish Fay (Iolanthe)

20   Oh, Gentlemen, Listen, I Pray (Trial by Jury)

182   Oh, Goddess Wise (Princess Ida)

94   Oh, Is There Not One Maiden Breast (The Pirates of Penzance)

317   On the Day When I Was Wedded (The Gondoliers)

114   The Policeman's Song (The Pirates of Penzance)

98   Poor Wand'ring One (The Pirates of Penzance)

142   Prithee, Pretty Maiden (Patience)

66   Refrain, Audacious Tar (H.M.S. Pinafore)

297   Rising Early in the Morning (The Gondoliers)

144   Silver'd Is the Raven Hair (Patience)

76   A Simple Sailor Lowly Born (H.M.S. Pinafore)

328   So Ends My Dream (The Grand Duke)

55   Sorry Her Lot Who Loves Too Well (H.M.S. Pinafore)

205   The Sun, Whose Rays Are All Ablaze (The Mikado)

304   Take a Pair of Sparkling Eyes (The Gondoliers)

232   There Is Beauty in the Bellow of the Blast (The Mikado)

308   There Lived a King (The Gondoliers)

199   Three Little Maids from School Are We (The Mikado)

23   Time Was, When Love and I (The Sorcerer)

244   To a Garden Full of Posies (Ruddigore)

124   Twenty Love-Sick Maidens We (Patience)

185   A Wand'ring Minstrel I (The Mikado)

271   Were I Thy Bride (The Yeoman of the Guard)

40   We Sail the Ocean Blue (H.M.S. Pinafore)

291   When a Merry Maiden Marries (The Gondoliers)

158   When All Night Long a Chap Remains (Iolanthe)

162   When Britain Really Ruled the Waves (Iolanthe)

17   When First My Old, Old Love I Knew (Trial By Jury)

87   When Frederic Was a Little Lad (The Pirates of Penzance)

132   When I First Put This Uniform On (Patience)

62   When I Was a Lad I Served a Term (H.M.S. Pinafore)

155   When I Went to the Bar as a Very Young Man (Iolanthe)

250   When Maiden Loves, She Sits and Sighs (The Yeoman of the Guard)

230   Willow, Tit-Willow (The Mikado)

117   With Cat-Like Tread, Upon Our Prey We Steal (The Pirates of Penzance)

SIR WILLIAM SCHWENCK GILBERT (1836-1911)
SIR ARTHUR SEYMOUR SULLIVAN (1842-1900)

The names Gilbert and Sullivan are not only synonymous with operetta, they are nearly inseparable one from the other. The 14 operettas the pair produced, virtually the only English operettas of the era that have survived, are the principal works by which the two are remembered, despite the fact that both men had extensive careers apart from their partnership. So magical were the products of their artistic collaboration that the operettas have remained in the repertoire since they first appeared, often in productions that adhere as closely as possible to the performances that the authors directed in London over a century ago. Companies devoted solely to the works of Gilbert and Sullivan continue to flourish around the world, with many players calling themselves "Savoyards," in homage to the famous Savoy Theatre, which was built to house their productions.

The magic of the eight Savoy operas (later designated as operettas), and the six which opened in other theatres, was due to equally important contributions from Gilbert and Sullivan. Gilbert, for his part, created librettos that mixed fantastical, ridiculous plots populated by comically flawed characters, with critical commentaries on the foibles and failings of British society and government. Sullivan held up his end of the partnership by providing remarkably balanced, irrepressible melodies that softened the impact of Gilbert's social criticisms, and at the same time, highlighted them. As individuals, Gilbert and Sullivan were as different as their respective contributions to the partnership.

Sir William Schwenck Gilbert, knighted in 1907 and acknowledged as one of the great English literary figures of his age, was an upright, proper gentleman, almost rigid in character. For all his personal pomposity, his greatest delight was in things ridiculous. His views on the silly side of life are best expressed by a line he gave to the character Jack Point in *The Yeomen of the Guard:* "...there is humour in all things, and the truest philosophy is that which teaches us to find it and make the most of it." Gilbert loved to create worlds in which characters and situations were the opposite of what they seemed, a realm he referred to as Topsy-Turvydom. His delight in creating a topsy-turvy world is evident throughout the operettas, most of which can be traced to stories or situations Gilbert created in his *Bab Ballads*, poems dubbed with his childhood nickname to give them a catchy title. He illustrated these works with drawings, as he later would illustrate his librettos.

Gilbert's childhood surfaced in one of the vehicles he used for these crazy twists of plot as well, as he often had his characters discovering that they had been kidnapped in infancy and raised by strangers. Gilbert himself was kidnapped from the care of a nanny at age two while his family was traveling in Naples. He was returned after a ransom was paid. The incident, perhaps combined with a cold unhappy, home life that ended with his parents parting company when Gilbert was 19, raised the nagging question of how his life might have been different had he been raised by someone else.

Arthur Seymour Sullivan, knighted in 1883, wanted to be respected and remembered for his "serious" works. His musical talent was recognized at an early age, his music first appearing in print when he was 13. Arthur won large scholarships in his teens that allowed him to study in Leipzig for several years. Although apparently an agnostic, he took several positions as a church organist, and composed quite a few hymns, including "Onward Christian Soldiers" and the standard British setting of "It Came upon a Midnight Clear" (a different tune from its American counterpart). But Sullivan's serious music was largely thought to be too weighty and ponderous, and even a bit stilted. His gift for melody found its freest expression in the operetta genre. Among Sullivan's most important contributions to "serious" music are the discoveries he made, with Sir George Grove, of two lost symphonies by Franz Schubert, as well as finding Schubert's incidental music for the play *Rosamunde*.

Where Gilbert was upright and uptight, Sullivan was a libertarian. Gilbert was tall and fair-haired; Sullivan was short, dark haired and fairly round. He was fond of the physical pleasures of life, smoking heavily, drinking and eating with abandon. While Gilbert was a devoted, proper husband, Sullivan never married, choosing instead to indulge in frequent amorous encounters. He spent his last 20 years with Mrs. Mary Frances Reynolds, an American estranged from her husband.

Gilbert and Sullivan's work brought them to each other's attention years before they actually began to work together. In 1867 Gilbert, who was writing magazine copy and working on the *Bab Ballads* at the time, wrote a review of *Cox and Box*, Sullivan's first comic opera. He found Sullivan's music too high class for the plot to which it was attached. This complaint would resurface during their collaboration. In March, 1869, a revival of Sullivan's *Cox and Box* appeared on the same bill as Gilbert's *No Cards*, with music by German Reed. This was the first time their names appeared together on the same playbill. In November of that same year Sullivan's close friend Fred Clay collaborated with Gilbert on a musical entertainment entitled *Ages Ago*. The piece was dedicated to Sullivan. It was during rehearsals for this production that Gilbert and Sullivan are believed finally to have met for the first time. The two men then met numerous times at gatherings of mutual friends, but were not disposed to become friends themselves, being of such different temperaments.

Gilbert and Sullivan were approached by German Reed about working on a joint production in 1870, but Sullivan declined. When they were approached again in 1871, both were free to commit to the project. Their first operetta, *Thespis or The Gods Grown Old*, opened on Boxing Day 1871. Opening night was a fiasco of delays and problems, with the final curtain falling after midnight. Eventually the show pulled together and ran for 64 performances. Sullivan was embarrassed by the piece in his later years. Although Gilbert's libretto has survived, the music was lost during Sullivan's lifetime, perhaps deliberately. When asked what had happened to the music, Sullivan replied that much of it was in his later works. When *Thespis* closed, Gilbert and Sullivan went back to their respective lives.

It was impresario Richard D'Oyly Carte who served as the catalyst that brought Gilbert and Sullivan together again for *Trial By Jury* (1875). The popular success of this second collaboration, and Carte's shrewd management, kept the team writing together for the next 15 years. *The Sorcerer* appeared in 1877, followed by the wildly successful *H.M.S. Pinafore* (1878). *Pinafore* was so successful in the U.S. in unauthorized, pirated productions, that Carte decided to premiere *The Pirates of Penzance* (1879) in New York, creating another international hit. *Patience* was the next new G&S show to open in London, in 1881.

With the big revenues created by *Pinafore*, Gilbert, Sullivan and D'Oyly Carte each contributed £1,000 to form a partnership. Gilbert and Sullivan agreed to provide a new operetta as required, on six months notice. Their shows toured extensively throughout the British Isles under the title Mr. D'Oyly Carte's Company. Carte's dream of devoting a venue to English operetta came to fruition in 1881 with his newly built Savoy Theatre, built on the ground where the Palace of the Savoy had been erected in 1240. This venue would serve as the official home to Gilbert & Sullivan productions for the next 80 years. The partnership produced *Iolanthe* in 1882 and *Princess Ida* in 1884, but both were disappointments. They didn't achieve another big hit until *The Mikado* in 1885. *Ruddigore* (1887), a mediocre success, was followed by *The Yeomen of the Guard* (1888), a better success. Gilbert & Sullivan's last huge hit was *The Gondoliers* in 1889, which almost equaled the popularity of *The Mikado*.

The partnership between writer, composer and manager was both the source of tremendous success and ongoing frustration. Gilbert felt as though he was being forced by the public to continue writing in a style that he had outgrown. Sullivan was still devoted to the idea of creating serious works, and continued composing cantatas and other such works. Gilbert was completely uninterested in serving as librettist for Sullivan's serious opera projects. These ongoing tensions, combined with wildly different personalities and lifestyles, were finally vented through an unrelated issue in what is known as The Carpet Quarrel. When D'Oyly Carte purchased new carpeting for the theatre, Gilbert objected to what he thought was the outrageous cost. Sullivan took Carte's side in the argument, which actually ended in court, a move that brought all of the simmering tensions to a full boil. The writers parted company bitterly after the premiere of *The Gondoliers* (1889). The rift was patched, if not thoroughly repaired, and the two came together again for *Utopia Limited* (1893) and *The Grand Duke* (1896). Neither were particularly successful.

After *The Grand Duke* they parted company for the last time, Gilbert returned to writing plays and Sullivan fulfilled a lifelong ambition in composing an opera, *Ivanhoe* (1891), and a few more operettas with other librettists. Although the operettas continued in revivals, there would be no new works. Sullivan's days of successes were effectively over. He spent a great deal of time gambling in Monte Carlo. His health was failing, causing him tremendous pain and forcing him to rely on morphine to get through a day. He died in London on November 22, 1900 from bronchitis and general poor health. Sullivan's funeral at St. Paul's Cathedral drew an enormous crowd. Richard D'Oyly Carte died four months later, in 1901. In his post G&S playwriting, Gilbert finally found the new style of writing he was searching for in his last work, *The Hooligan*, a strong dramatic piece produced four months before his death. He died on May 29, 1911, while trying to save a young woman from drowning.

The D'Oyly Carte Opera Company held the monopoly on Gilbert and Sullivan's collaborations until 1961. Today Gilbert and Sullivan's operettas are heard throughout the world, often presented by companies devoted solely to their performance. The D'Oyly Carte Trust, Ltd. is still active, presenting operas once again in the London's Savoy Theatre as of 2000. Snippets and excerpts of the various works have appeared in some unlikely film and television productions. Bits of Mikado can be seen or heard in the films *Foul Play* (1978), *The Bad News Bears Go to Japan* (1978), *Chariots of Fire* (1981), *A Passage to India* (1984), and an episode of the television series *Magnum P.I.* Excerpts from *Pinafore* turned up in *Star Trek: Insurrection* (1998). In 1999, director Mike Leigh created a full length, feature film devoted to the creation of *The Mikado*, calling it *Topsy-Turvy*. Clearly our fascination with Gilbert and Sullivan is far from over.

— Elaine Schmidt

TRIAL BY JURY

First produced at the Royalty Theatre, London, on March 25, 1875, with a run of 131 performances. It appeared on a triple bill, with Offenbach's *La Périchole* as the centerpiece. It was an immediate hit, and soon became the main attraction. Today *Trial By Jury* is often performed with *H.M.S. Pinafore*.

Sullivan's only one-act opera and the pair's only collaborative work with no spoken dialog, *Trial by Jury* opens on a court-room where a trial for breach of marital promise is about to begin. An usher admonishes the jurors to be impartial but then tells them to listen with sympathy to Angelina, the spurned bride, and to ignore the story of Edwin, the would-be groom. The judge enters, promptly singing his entire life's story for the court. When the bridesmaids enter, dressed for the wedding, the judge immediately sends a note to one of them, professing his love for her. Angelina enters shortly, in her wedding gown. The judge immediately has the amorous note taken from the bridesmaid and given to Angelina. The jurors shake their fists at Edwin. They make it clear they are not interested as he sings "When First My Old, Old Love I Knew," explaining how he fell in and out of love with Angelina. The trial quickly degenerates into a weeping bride clinging to the groom who still rejects her. Edwin makes his plea to the jury with "Oh, Gentlemen, Listen, I Pray." The judge ends the trial and the operetta by announcing that he will marry Angelina himself.

THE SORCERER

First produced at the Opéra Comique, London, on November 17, 1877, with a run of 178 performances.

The village of Ploverleigh is percolating with affection as this satire on Victorian society opens. Aline Sangazure sings "Happy Young Heart," glorying in engagement to Alexis Poindextre of the Grenadier Guards. Villager Constance Partlet harbors secret feelings for Dr. Daly, the Vicar. Daly sings "Time Was, When Love and I" oblivious of Constance's feelings. Constance's mother, meanwhile, has her eye on the Notary. Aline and Alexis, hoping to share their loving bliss with the entire village, hire a sorcerer to drug the community with a love-at-first-sight potion. The sorcerer introduces himself with "My Name Is John Wellington Wells," and is then hired. The potion is administered through tea at a village picnic. Everyone but the young lovers and the sorcerer drink the potion-spiked tea and fall into a deep sleep. When they awake, they will each fall in love with the first person they see.

As midnight strikes the villagers begin to awaken, immediately falling head-over-heels in love with the first person they happen to spot. Seeing the potion's effects, Alexis asks Aline to drink the potion, to deepen their love for each other. She refuses, causing a quarrel. Eventually she agrees, but spots Dr. Daly immediately afterward and falls in love with him instead of her betrothed Alexis. The potion-induced romances have made a mess of things. Alexis' father, Sir Marmaduke has fallen for Mrs. Partlet, while Lady Sangazure has become smitten with Mr. Wells and Constance with the Notary. It becomes apparent that either Alexis or Mr. Wells must give his life to the forces of evil to break the spell. Neither is willing so a vote is taken. The sorcerer loses and is swallowed up by the earth as a gong sounds. The potion's spell is broken and the villagers return to their original affections.

H.M.S. PINAFORE

or The Lass that Loved a Sailor

First produced at the Opéra Comique, London, on May 25, 1878, with a run of 571 performances.

On the *Pinafore*, anchored off Portsmouth, the crew is singing a proud rendition of "We Sail the Ocean Blue" as this satire on British class distinctions and military life opens. A woman named Little Buttercup comes aboard to sell them ribbons and lace for their sweethearts, introducing herself with "I'm Called Little Buttercup." Despite her merry demeanor, she carries a mysterious secret. Sailor Ralph Rackstraw, the smartest man in the fleet, declares his love for a young maiden with "A Maiden Fair to See." That maiden, unfortunately, is the captain's daughter. The sailor Dick Deadeye appears with the unkindly explanation that captain's daughters do not marry mere sailors. Enter the Captain, with the introductory "I Am the Captain of the Pinafore." He explains to Little Buttercup that he is worried because his daughter, Josephine, has refused to marry the Sir Joseph Porter, First Lord of the Admiralty. Josephine herself enters, singing "Sorry Her Lot Who Loves Too Well," thus declaring her love for a sailor aboard Pinafore. After her father explains the class issues involved with her romance she promises to forsake the sailor and reconsider Sir Joseph. Sir Joseph himself enters with "I Am the Monarch of the Sea" and "When I Was a Lad I Served a Term." Ralph finally summons the courage to confess his love to Josephine, only to have her respond coldly with "Refrain, Audacious Tar." A heartbroken Ralph threatens to shoot himself, but Josephine relents and confesses that she indeed loves him.

As Act II begins, the Captain paces the deck by night and singing "Fair Moon, to Thee I Sing." He confesses his love for Little Buttercup but quickly explains that their different social positions make a relationship impossible. Little Buttercup cryptically advises him not to be too sure of that. Sir Joseph and Josephine enter. Sir Joseph is convinced that Josephine is intimidated by his high social standing, all the while she plots her elopement with Ralph. She sings "A Simple Sailor Lowly Born." The evil Dick Deadeye informs the Captain of Josephine's upcoming elopement, allowing the Captain to stop the marriage. But the crew steps in on Ralph's behalf, assuring the Captain "He Is an Englishman!" The Captain curses at this, which brings Sir Joseph out of the woodwork to berate him for speaking so rudely to a British sailor. Once Sir Joseph realizes his love intended to elope with Ralph, he orders the young sailor confined below decks. At the last moment Little Buttercup brings out the truth of her mysterious secret. Apparently she once worked as a nanny of sorts, and made a terrible mistake through which two babies were mixed up. Those babies were the Captain and Ralph. So, in fact, the Captain is a mere sailor and Ralph is the Captain. Her news rings in a happy ending, as Ralph and Josephine as well as the Captain and Little Buttercup are freed from social restrictions and free to marry.

THE PIRATES OF PENZANCE
or The Slave of Duty
One performance, for copyright purposes, was given on December 30, 1879 at the Royal Bijou Theatre in Paighton, Devonshire. It opened officially for a run in New York at the Fifth Avenue Theatre on December 31, 1879. The London premiere was at the Opéra Comique on April 3, 1880, with a run of 363 performances.

Pirate festivities on the Cornwall coast open this satire on British military and constabulary, celebrating the completion of young Frederic's pirate internship. But Frederic is dejected. His situation is explained by Ruth, who had been his nursemaid, with "When Frederic Was a Little Lad." It seems that Ruth, being quite hard of hearing, mistook Frederic's father's instruction to apprentice him as a pilot and instead set him up as a pirate. The heartbroken Frederic he must, for duty's sake, return to the honest world and work to end piracy even though this means betraying his pirate friends. He begs the pirates to give up their life of crime but they decline to the tune of "I Am a Pirate King." Ruth begs Frederic to take her with him, as he has never seen another woman and considers the aging Ruth to be beautiful. Just then a party of beautiful young maidens appear for a picnic who are shocked to find a pirate in their midst. He begs "Oh, Is There Not One Maiden Breast," hoping one of them will accept him. Just when it appears that all will reject him, Mabel appears and bravely offers him her heart with "Poor Wandering One." The other pirates spot the lovely maidens and creep in to kidnap them. The girls' father appears, announcing "I Am the Very Model of a Modern Major-General," hoping to foil the pirates' plans of marriage. When that fails he plays on his knowledge that Pirates of Penzance are orphans and are always tenderhearted toward other orphans. He explains that he too is an orphan and would be lost and lonely without his daughters. The pirates relent and the Major-General, Frederic and the girls depart, leaving poor Ruth with the pirates.

Act II opens in a ruined chapel, where the Major-General confesses to Frederic and Mabel that he is not actually an orphan. Frederic explains his plans to put the pirates out of business, and is in the process of proposing to Mabel when policemen arrive on their way to conquer the pirates themselves. They are just describing their grand plans when Ruth and the Pirate King arrive with a most ingenious paradox. Apparently Frederic was born on a leap-year day, so he won't actually reach his 21st birthday until 1940. Therefore he is still the pirates' apprentice. Always a slave to duty, Frederic returns to his pirate life, where honor forces him to tell the pirates that the Major-General is not an orphan. The policemen reappear and sing "The Policeman's Song" as they reluctantly prepare to arrest the pirates. The pirates meanwhile can be heard sneaking up on the Major-General singing "With Cat-Like Tread Upon Our Prey We Steal." Just as the pirates are about to do in the Major-General, the policemen leap to his defense, only to be defeated almost immediately. They are about to be killed when the police pull Union Jacks from their pockets and command the pirates to stand down in the name of Queen Victoria. The pirates, who love their Queen, comply. Ruth puts everything to rights by explaining that the pirates are actually noblemen who have gone wrong. They are immediately forgiven and given back their titles. Frederic and Mabel reunite and the Major-General asks the pirate/nobles to marry his daughters.

PATIENCE
or Bunthorne's Bride
First produced at the Opéra Comique, London, on April 23, 1881, with a run of 578 performances.

A bevy of lovely maidens are gathered at Bunthorne's Castle, singing "Twenty Love-Sick Maidens We" as this satire on the aesthetic movement opens. All of the maidens are smitten with the poet Reginald Bunthorne, who has secret feelings for Patience, the village milkmaid. Only Lady Jane realizes the truth of his affections. Patience wonders why people in love never look quite healthy, so the maidens explain that they have always been in love. In fact they were once engaged to the Thirty-Fifth Dragoon Guards, who immediately march on stage followed by their Colonel. But they are no match, in the maidens' eyes, for poet Bunthorne. Bunthorne himself enters, seemingly engrossed in a poem he is composing but slyly listening to everything. As he reads his poem aloud the maidens become even more smitten with him. The Colonel sings "When I First Put This Uniform On," remembering how he used to think a uniform would make a man irresistible. Bunthorne sings "Am I Alone and Unobserved?" to explain that he is an aesthetic fake. He then makes romantic overtures to Patience, who is not interested in love. But the maidens explain to Patience that love is a duty and she decides to fall in love. Another poet, Archibald Grosvenor arrives and proposes to her with "Prithee, Pretty Maiden." He reminds Patience that he is the boy she had loved as a child. Bunthorne, meanwhile, has decided to raffle himself off, only to be stopped at the last minute by Patience's offer to marry him. She indeed loves Grosvenor, but believes that she can only love unselfishly if she has no feelings for the object of her affections. The maidens decide to turn their affections back to the Dragoons, only to redirect them to Grosvenor the moment he appears.

As Act II begins, Lady Jane is deciding to forsake the Dragoons in favor of Bunthorne. But she feels that they ought to marry in a hurry, explaining with "Silver'd Is the Woman's Hair," that she is not getting any younger. Grosvenor enters, with the smitten maidens traipsing along behind, making it clear that his heart remains with Patience. Patience now realizes that she should be with Grosvenor whom she loves, but duty requires that she keep her promise to marry Bunthorne. She sings a melancholy "Love Is a Plaintive Song." The rival poets are wildly jealous of each other by this point. Bunthorne demands that Grosvenor cease being an aesthetic and Grosvenor eventually agrees. Bunthorne decides to reform his unpleasant traits. Patience decides that loving the now perfect Bunthorne is hardly unselfish, so she feels free to love Grosvenor, who has become a common-place, everyday man, as per his agreement with Bunthorne. Lady Jane and the maidens all marry Dragoons, leaving Bunthorne alone with his false poetry.

IOLANTHE

or The Peer and the Peri

First produced at the Savoy Theatre, London, on November 25, 1882, with a run of 398 performances.

The lovely fairy women of Arcadia are unhappy in this satire on the House of Lords, because the Fairy Queen has banished Iolanthe for marrying a human. The Queen who is secretly in love with a human named Private Willis, eventually relents and pardons Iolanthe. Iolanthe returns, looking like a young woman of 17 even though she has a 25-year-old son. Her son, Strephon, is planning to marry Phyllis, the young ward of the Lord Chancellor. But the couple has not received his blessing. The Lord Chancellor and a chorus of nobles march about demanding respect and fanfare. The Lord Chancellor further exalts their station by singing "The Law Is the True Embodiment." He loves Phyllis himself, but fearing the marriage would not be proper he asks the nobles if one of them might marry her. Phyllis announces her objection, adding that her heart has already been given to another. Strephon enters at that moment and announces that he is the object of her affection. The Chancellor sings "When I Went to the Bar," dashing Strephon's hopes. When Strephon tells his mother of these goings on, she takes him in her arms to comfort him. Phyllis sees Strephon in the arms of this apparent 17-year-old. Certain she has been betrayed, she becomes engaged to two noblemen. As the act comes to an end, the Fairy Queen decides to send Strephon to Parliament to make nobles out of commoners and generally make life miserable for the Lord Chancellor and the other nobles.

Act II opens on the Westminster Palace Yard, with Private Willis singing "When All Night Long a Chap Remains." Strephon has caused an uproar in Parliament, whimsically passing pointless laws. The peers, singing "When Britain Really Ruled the Waves," appeal to the fairies. They offer no help but find the peers quite attractive. Despite her love for Willis, the Fairy Queen sings "Oh Foolish Fay" to scold them for even thinking about marrying mortals. Phyllis meanwhile finds her two fiancées equally uninteresting so she tells them she will choose the one who will forsake his title and give his wealth to the Irish tenantry, which neither will do. Strephon eventually convinces Phyllis that Iolanthe is really his mother and they plan to marry immediately. The Lord Chancellor who "sings" the brilliant patter-song "Love, Unrequited, Robs Me of My Rest," has in the meantime convinced himself that it be acceptable for him to marry his ward. But Iolanthe steps to confess that she is his long-lost wife. The Queen is about to order Iolanthe's execution for this marriage, when the fairies step forward to announce they have all married nobles. To save them all from execution, the Lord Chancellor rewrites the law so that any fairy who does not marry a mortal will be condemned to death. The Queen happily marries Private Willis to save her own life. Wings sprout from the nobles' shoulders as the House of Peers becomes the House of Peri.

PRINCESS IDA

or Castle Adamant

First produced at the Savoy Theatre, London, on January 5, 1884, with a run of 246 performances. *Princess Ida* is Gilbert and Sullivan's only three-act operetta.

This satire on women's suffrage and Darwin's evolutionary theories, opens on a scene of great expectation. Prince Hilarion awaits the arrival of Princess Ida, to whom he has been betrothed since infancy. But her father, King Gama, arrives without her. The King sings "If You Give Me Your Attention" to explain to the Prince and his father King Hildebrand, that Princess Ida is now running a school for girls at Castle Adamant. There they study the classics and the villainy of men. The Princess sings "Oh, Goddess Wise" in reverie of Minerva the Goddess of Wisdom. Hildebrand and Hilarion decide to hold Gama and his three sons as hostages while they storm the Castle Adamant to claim the Princess.

Hilarion and two friends scale the castle wall and disguise themselves in women's clothing. With several of the women aware of the men, and keeping their secret, the three pull off the ruse for a time. But after drinking a bit too much one of the men gives up the secret. Princess Ida orders the men's arrest. But King Hildebrand has massed his troops outside the castle walls to force Ida to make good on the betrothal. He gives her twenty-four hours to make up her mind, threatening to raze the castle and hang her brothers and father if she declines.

The Princess decides to fight, but her students are in terror of hurting someone so they refuse. Meanwhile King Hildebrand has decided that fighting women is in poor form, so he has Ida's brothers brought from his castle to fight for the women against Prince Hilarion and his two friends. Hilarion and company win. Princess Ida marries Hilarion, and two of her colleagues marry his friends. Lady Blanche is left to fulfill her dream of running the school and the curtain falls.

THE MIKADO
or The Town of Titipu
First produced at the Savoy Theatre, London, on March 14, 1885, with a run of 672 performances.

The setting for this most popular of Savoy operettas is the courtyard of the Japanese Lord High Executioner in the town of Titipu. Handsome Nanki-Poo runs in looking for the lovely Yum-Yum, adopting a disguise with "A Wand'ring Minstrel I." He has loved Yum-Yum for a long time and now that Ko-Ko, Yum-Yum's guardian and fiancée, is to be beheaded he sees his opportunity. But no. Ko-Ko himself enters and announces his new appointment as Lord High Executioner, singing "As Some Day It May Happen." As he discusses his wedding plans, Yum-Yum and two school-mates enter singing "Three Little Maids From School Are We." Nanki-Poo apologizes to Ko-Ko for being in love Yum-Yum, receiving forgiveness. Later Yum-Yum confesses to Nanki-Poo that she does not love Ko-Ko. Nanki-Poo confesses that he is actually son of the Mikado and is traveling in disguise to avoid marrying an elderly woman who mistook his good nature for affectionate advances. The Mikado meanwhile has sent word to Ko-Ko that if he doesn't execute someone soon his title will be abolished and the town reduced to a mere village. Ko-Ko spots Nanki-Poo about to end his life over his hopeless love, and asks if he might execute him since the lad is about do himself in anyway. Nanki-Poo agrees on the condition that he be allowed to marry Yum-Yum and live with her for one month before the execution. Ko-Ko agrees, being a more practical than romantic man. When Katisha, the elderly woman who wants to marry Nanki-Poo, arrives and tries to tell everyone of his true identity, she is ignored.

Act two opens on the preparations for Yum-Yum's wedding. Obsessed with her own beauty, she sings "The Sun, Whose Rays Are All Ablaze." But happiness dims when Ko-Ko learns that by law she, as the widow of Nanki-Poo, must be buried alive following his execution. A bribe to the Pooh-Bah (also known as the Lord High Everything Else) to fake a certificate of execution seems the best course of action until the Mikado arrives to a chorus of "Mi-Ya-Sa-Ma." He sings "The Mikado's Song" and checks on the execution. Katisha sees the execution certificate and tells the Mikado that his son has been executed, the Mikado promises punishment to all involved. Ko-Ko goes to Nanki-Poo for advice. Nanki-Poo sings "When Flowers That Bloom in the Spring" and advises him to marry Katisha. Katisha sings the dramatic "Alone, and Yet Alive." Ko-Ko woos Katisha with "Willow, Tit-Willow" which segues into their duet, "There Is Beauty in the Bellow of the Blast." Nanki-Poo, now free from Katisha's clutches, comes out of hiding and introduces the Mikado to his new daughter-in-law and thus ends the threat of punishment and the operetta.

RUDDIGORE
or The Witch's Curse
First produced at the Savoy Theatre, London, on March 14, 1885 for a run of 288 performances.

The professional bridesmaids in the Cornish village of Rederring are antsy for work. The lovely Rose Maybud is the most likely candidate, but keeps rejecting suitors. She sings "If Somebody There Chanced to Be," explaining that she is waiting for the right person. Rose's Aunt Hannah tells of Sir Roderic Murgatroyd of Ruddigore, her lost love. Roderic defied the curse of the Murgatroyd heirs, which condemns them to commit a crime each day or perish, and died on their wedding day. The shy Robin Oakapple, who is really Sir Ruthven Murgatroyd, appears. Despard Murgatroyd , has assumed the title and is living the obligatory life of crime. Robin explains that he is too shy to approach Rose with "My Boy, You May Take It From Me." Robin's half brother, a sailor named Richard, offers to woo Rose on Robin's behalf, but falls madly in love with her and woos her for himself instead. When Robin learns of this betrayal he poisons Rose's mind against sailors and she turns her affections to him. At this point Mad Margaret enters singing "A Garden Full of Posies." Driven to insanity by Despard, she is wildly jealous of Rose who reassures her. The plot thickens when Robin reveals himself as Despard's older brother, whom all thought was dead. Robin's title is restored and Rose leaves him for Despard. But Despard spurns her, going back to Margaret. Rose returns to Richard and Robin collapses.

Act II opens with a haggard Sir Ruthven in the picture gallery of his castle, looking for a crime to commit and singing "Henceforth All the Crimes." Rose and Richard have come to ask permission to marry and Ruthven threatens to imprison Rose as his crime of the day. Richard pulls out a Union Jack, which of course even the worst of criminals cannot ignore, and the two leave safely. At this point the portraits of the previously cursed Murgatroyds come to life to remind Ruthven what will happen if he fails to commit a crime. Ruthven wearily sends someone off to kidnap a maiden on his behalf, which brings Hannah to the castle. In the meantime Despard and Margaret, now school masters, arrive to encourage Ruthven to reform. They add that under the law Ruthven is responsible for Despard's crime as well as his own. Ruthven vows to reform, no matter what the consequences. With Hannah in the room, Ruthven calls upon the picture of his Uncle Roderic to help him. Roderic's picture comes to life and he spots Hannah. Ruthven leaves, contemplating his predicament. But the day is saved when Ruthven rushes back in with a brainstorm. Failing to commit a crime each day while knowing the sentence for such action is death, he reasons, is tantamount to suicide. Since suicide is a crime in and of itself, Sir Roderic should never have died. This means that all concerned may pair off as they see fit and thus ends the curse and the operetta.

THE YEOMAN OF THE GUARD
or The Merryman and His Maid
First produced at the Savoy Theatre, London, on October 3, 1888 for a run of 423 performances.

The year is fifteen-hundred-and-something. Young Phoebe Meryll ponders the heartbreaks of love singing, "When Maiden Loves, She Sits and Sighs." She is pining for the dashing Colonel Fairfax who sits in the Tower of London awaiting execution for the crime of sorcery, singing "Is Life a Boon?" He was accused of the crime by his scheming cousin. Should he die without a wife, Fairfax explains to the Lieutenant, his title and wealth transfer to the cousin. He begs the Lieutenant to marry him to the poorest woman that can be found so that she might inherit his name and wealth instead. Meanwhile Wilfred, Head Jailor and Assistant Tormentor of the Tower of London, has eyes for Phoebe. While she once thought him fine, she has since become enamored of the Colonel and will have nothing to with Wilfred. Jester Jack Point and singer Elsie Maynard enter singing "I Have a Song to Sing, O!" A less than appreciative crowd threatens to mob them but the Lieutenant saves them, immediately marrying Elsie to Fairfax. Jack describes his profession with "I've a Jibe and a Joke." Meanwhile, Phoebe has come up with a plan. She flirts with Wilfrid, singing "Were I Thy Bride." She steals his keys just long enough for her father to free Fairfax. Wilfrid is barely gone when Fairfax appears in the uniform of the Yeoman of the Guard, posing as the son of Sergeant Meryll. As Phoebe and her "brother" give each other an uncommonly affectionate greeting, the bells toll the hour of the execution. Guards rush back with the news that Fairfax has escaped.

Act II finds Jack Point feeling regret for allowing Elsie to marry Fairfax. It seemed a better idea when Fairfax was about to die, since Jack wanted to marry Elsie himself and figured Fairfax's money would be welcome. He advises Wilfrid on the hazards of jesting with "Oh! A Private Buffoon Is a Light-Hearted Loon." The newly freed Fairfax is putting the fidelity of his new wife to the test, masquerading as Leonard Meryll. Jack and Wilfrid conspire to fake Fairfax's death, saying that they shot the Colonel as he dove into the river. With Fairfax thought dead, Jack proposes to Elsie, who rejects him. Fairfax sings "Free From His Fetters Grim" wondering who his new bride might be, only to discover moments later that his bride is Elsie. Phoebe, distraught over loosing Fairfax tells Wilfrid of the escape and disguise. Wilfrid forces her to marry him to keep the secret. Suddenly the real Leonard appears with an official pardon for Fairfax. Elsie, at first heartbroken to learn that her real husband is alive is delighted when it is revealed that her beloved Leonard is really Fairfax and therefore they are married. Jack, the only one left without a spouse, falls to the ground in a faint.

THE GONDOLIERS
or The King of Barataria
First produced at the Savoy Theatre, London, on December 7, 1889 for a run of 554 performances.

Twenty four Venetian flower girls are arranging the bouquets they will present to Marco and Giuseppe, the handsomest of all the gondoliers, in hopes of snagging a marriage proposal. The gondoliers decide to choose their brides via a game of blind man's bluff. Happily they end up with girls they most wanted – Marco with Gianetta and Giuseppe with Tessa. A gondola arrives and "The Duke of Plaza-Toro" is sung by the penniless character of the same name. He tells his daughter, Casilda, that she was married by proxy to the King of Barataria when she was just an infant. Casilda however loves the drummer Luiz. The King is informed by the Grand Inquisitor, singing "No Possible Doubt Whatever," that the King was kidnapped, raised by a gondolier and is now working as a gondolier in Venice. The two newlywed couples return singing, "When a Merry Maiden Marries." The Grand Inquisitor is certain that one of the men is King, although he can't say which, and takes them back to Barataria. They will rule jointly until the King's old nursemaid, who is the mother of Luiz, can determine which is the real King.

Act II opens in the Court of Barataria, where the democratic leanings of the joint Kings are immediately apparent. The Kings sing "Rising Early in the Morning," as they toil all day for their kingdom. With "Take a Pair of Sparkling Eyes," they miss their brides. The brides appear, unable to bear the separation any longer. When the Grand Inquisitor arrives he sings "There Lived a King" to explain that this sort of thing had been tried once before to no good end. The Duke arrives with Casilda, who is technically married to one of the two Kings, and Luiz. The three brides ponder the predicament of their two husbands and Casilda's mother sings "On the Day When I Was Wedded," telling of her own marriage. The Grand Inquisitor brings in Inez, the nursemaid to identify the real King. She confesses that when the King was kidnapped she tricked the Grand Inquisitor by substituting her own son for the King and raising the young King herself. So the two Kings are gondoliers once again, each happily married to his love. Luiz and Casilda must be married, which suits them just fine.

UTOPIA LIMITED
or The Flowers of Progress
First produced at the Savoy Theatre, London, on October 7, 1893 for a run of 245 performances.

This mockery of Victorian society is set on a the fictitious South Pacific island of Utopia, where the King's daughter, Princess Zara, is about to return from school in Britain. Two wise men, Scaphio and Phantis, hold power over Utopia and its King. The two wise men tout their own virtues with "In Ev'ry Mental Lore." Tarara explains that as the Public Exploder he must explode anything or anyone denounced by Scaphio and Phantis. A scandal sheet called the *Palace Peeper* has accused the

King of terrible behavior and Tarara thinks it is time for an explosion. The King announces that due to public demand Utopia will be modeled after Great Britain, with Lady Sophy teaching the girls proper behavior. We learn that the King himself has written the scandal sheet, under orders from Scaphio and Phantis. Scaphio has promised Phantis to help him win Zara's heart. But one look at her and he is in love with her himself. Zara and Fitzbattleaxe interrupt, explaining that in Britain if two men love one woman they must duel to the death to decide who wins the woman. The King tells Zara of Scaphio and Phantis' power over him. She has conveniently brought "experts" from England to set Utopia to rights. As per their advice, the King incorporates himself. In fact everyone in Utopia is now a limited company. The King, dressed in British military attire, holds his first cabinet meeting. With Scaphio and Phantis grumbling about the Anglicization of Utopia, the King tells them he is a limited company and therefore immune to their control. They call in the Public Exploder and cook up a plot. The king tells Lady Sophy the truth about the *Palace Peeper* and about Scaphio and Phantis. But things are now too good in Utopia. There is no work for the Army or Navy, no disease for doctors to cure and no crime for lawyers to prosecute. So the King decides to follow the British system of Government by party saying, "No political measures will endure, because one party will assuredly undo all that the other party has done."

THE GRAND DUKE
or The Statutory Duel
First produced at the Savoy Theatre, London, on March 7, 1896 for a run of 123 performances. The pair's last collaboration, it was not performed again in London until it was heard in a concert performance at the same theater in 1975.

A sharp tongued commentary on everything from Queen Victoria's German roots to Carte's preoccupation with money and Sullivan's Irish heritage, this operetta opens on a marketplace in Speisesaal, the capitol of the Grand Duchy of Pfennig-Halbpfennig in 1750. A theatrical troupe, with a manager named Ernest Dummkopf, is celebrating in advance of the nuptials of the leading comedian Ludwig to Julia. The troupe members are part of a conspiracy to overthrow the Duke and put Dummkopf in his place. The Duke meanwhile, is planning his own wedding to the exceptionally wealthy Baroness von Krankenfeldt. Convolutions of plot, including the infant betrothal of the Duke and misinterpretations of a secret signal necessitate a duel. Traditional dueling is forbidden so a statutory duel takes place instead. The combatants draw cards, the higher card winning. The loser becomes "dead" for 24 hours. The winner is obliged to clear up all of the loser's debts and obligations before the "dead" person returns to life. Ernest and Ludwig duel, with Ludwig drawing an ace and winning. The Duke and Ludwig then duel, with Ludwig drawing another ace and winning again. Ludwig the Duke for twenty-four hairs, quickly changes the law to keep the "dead" losers "dead." This, of course, creates romantic mayhem since the "dead" cannot marry. The sorrowful Julia sings "So Ends My Dream." Just as the Prince of Monte Carlo arrives with his daughter to thoroughly muddy the waters, a notary points out that by law the ace is the lowest card. Since Ludwig won the duels with an ace, he is in fact the loser. The couples sort themselves back to rights and the curtain falls on the happy ending.

H.M.S. PINAFORE
Gilbert's "Bab" illustrations

"I'm called Little Buttercup," Buttercup and Captain Corcoran

Sister's, Cousins or Aunts "lightly tripping"

Dick Deadeye and Captain Corcoran

Sir Joseph at his desk

THE PIRATES OF PENZANCE
Gilbert's "Bab" Illustrations

The Modern Major-General

The Policeman's Song

Mabel sings "Poor Wand'ring One"

Ruth

THE MIKADO
Gilbert's "Bab" Illustrations"

Koko singing "Willow, Tit-Willow"

"The Sun, whose rays are all ablaze with ever-living glory"

Yum Yum and Koko

"His teeth, I've enacted, shall be extracted by terrified amateurs."

When First My Old, Old Love I Knew

TRIAL BY JURY

Words by W.S. Gilbert
Music by Arthur Sullivan

Oh, Gentlemen, Listen, I Pray

TRIAL BY JURY

Words by W.S. Gilbert
Music by Arthur Sullivan

BRIDESMAIDS CHORUS:
(rushing forward and kneeling to jury)

day, And loves that young la - dy to - mor - row! Con - sid - er the mor - al, we
day, And I'll mar - ry the oth - er to - mor - row! But this he is will - ing to

pray, Nor bring a young fel - low to sor - row, Who loves this young la - dy to -
say, If it will ap - pease her sor - row, He'll mar - ry this la - dy to -

DEFENDANT:

day, And loves that young la - dy to - mor - row! You
day, And he'll mar - ry the oth - er to - mor - row!

Time Was, When Love and I

THE SORCERER

Words by W.S. Gilbert
Music by Arthur Sullivan

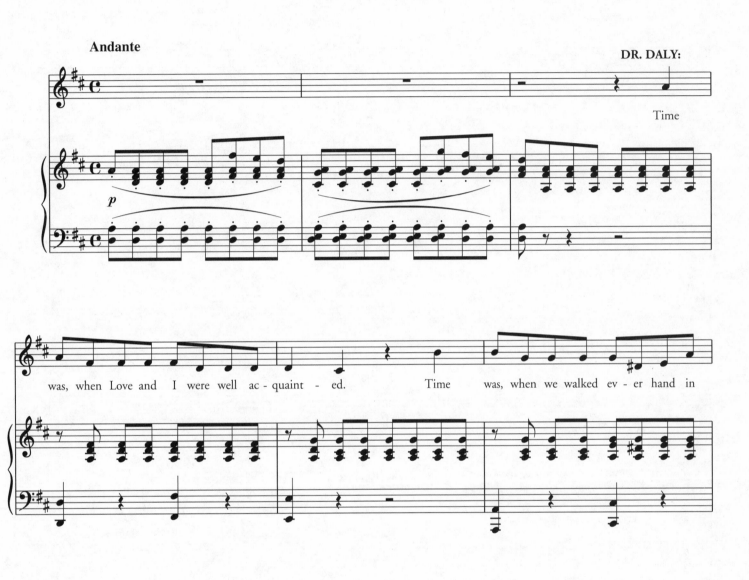

None bet-ter-loved than I in all the land! Time

was, when maid-ens of the no-blest sta-tion, For - sak-ing e - ven mil - i-tar-y

men, Would gaze up-on me, rapt in a-do-ra - tion— Ah

me, ah me, I was a fair young cu - rate then!

cresc.

[ad lib.]

colla voce

mf

Had I a head-ache? sighed _ the maids as-sem-bled; Had I a cold? welled forth the si-lent tear; Did I look pale? then half a par-ish trem-bled; And when I coughed all thought the end was near! I had no care— no jeal-ous doubts hung o'er me, For

opt.

Happy Young Heart
THE SORCERER

Words by W.S. Gilbert
Music by Arthur Sullivan

Tempo di Valse non troppo vivace

ALINE:

Oh, hap - py young heart! Comes thy young lord a -
Oh, mer - ry young heart! Bright are the days of

woo - ing, With
woo - ing! But

My Name Is John Wellington Wells

THE SORCERER

Words by W.S. Gilbert
Music by Arthur Sullivan

bless-ings and curs-es, And ev-er-filled purs-es, In proph-e-cies, witch-es, and knells. _____ If you

want a proud foe to "make tracks"— _____ If you'd melt a rich un-cle in wax— _____ You've

but to look in On the res-i-dent Djinn, Num-ber sev-en-ty, Sim-mer-y

Axe. _____ We've a first-rate as-sort-ment of mag-ic; And for rais-ing a post-hu-mous

And, if you want it, he Makes a re - duc - tion on tak - ing a quan - ti - ty!

Oh! _____ If an - y - one an - y - thing lacks, _____ He'll

find it all read - y in stacks, _____ If he'll on - ly look in On the res - i - dent Djinn, Num - ber

sev - en - ty, Sim - mer - y Axe!

He can raise you hosts Of ghosts, And

that, with-out re - flec - tors; And creep - y things With wings, And

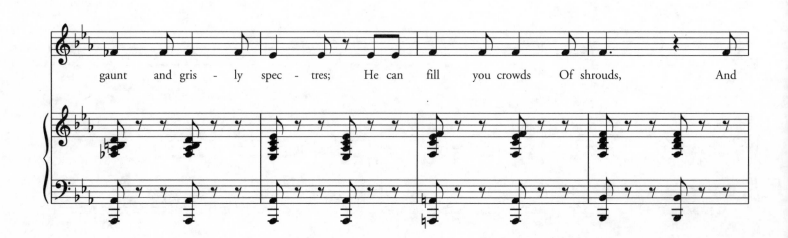

gaunt and gris - ly spec - tres; He can fill you crowds Of shrouds, And

hor-ri-fy you vast-ly; He can rack your brains With chains, _____ And

gib-ber-ings grim and ghast-ly! Then, if you plan it, he Chang-es or-gan-i-ty,

With an ur-ban-i-ty Full of sa-tan-i-ty, Vex-es hu-man-i-ty

With an in-an-i-ty Fa-tal to van-i-ty, Driv-ing your foes to the

We Sail the Ocean Blue

H.M.S. PINAFORE

Words by W.S. Gilbert
Music by Arthur Sullivan

Allegretto pesante

du - ty.   Our   sau - cy   ship's   a   beau - ty,   We're at -
du - ty.   Our   sau - cy   ship's   a   beau - ty,   We're at -

ten - tive   to   our   du - ty;   We're   so - ber   men   and
ten - tive   to   our   du - ty;   We're

true,   We   sail   the   o -   cean   blue.

I'm Called Little Buttercup

H.M.S. PINAFORE

Words by W.S. Gilbert
Music by Arthur Sullivan

pret - ty young sweet-hearts and wives. I've trea - cle and

tof - fee, I've tea and I've cof - fee, Soft tom - my and suc - cu -lent

chops; I've chick - ens and co - nies, and pret - ty po -

rall. *a tempo*

lo - nies, And ex - cel -lent pep - per - mint drops. Then

A Maiden Fair to See

H.M.S. PINAFORE

Words by W.S. Gilbert
Music by Arthur Sullivan

RALPH:

do her me-nial's du-ty. A suit-or, low-ly born, With

hope-less pas-sion torn, And poor, be-yond ___ de - ny - ing, Has

dared for her to pine, At whose ex - alt-ed shrine A world of wealth is

CHORUS:

sigh - ing. A world of wealth is sigh - ing.

RALPH:

Un - learn-ed he in aught Save

I Am the Captain of the Pinafore

H.M.S. PINAFORE

Words by W.S. Gilbert
Music by Arthur Sullivan

am   the   cap - tain   of the   *Pin - a - fore!* __ And a   right __ good __ cap - tain,
do   my   best   to   sat - is - fy   you   all __   And with   you __ we're __ quite   con -

CAPTAIN:

too! You're ver-y, ver-y good, And, be it un-der-stood, I com-
tent. You're ex-ceed-ing-ly po-lite, And I think it on-ly right To re-

CHORUS:

mand a ____ right good crew. We're ver-y, ver-y good, And,
turn the ____ com-pli-ment. We're ex-ceed-ing-ly po-lite, And he

CAPTAIN:

be it un-der-stood, He com-mands a ____ right good crew. Though re-
thinks it on-ly right To re-turn the ____ com-pli-ment. Bad

la-ted to a peer, I can hand, reef, and steer, Or ship a sel-a va-
lan-guage or a-buse, I nev-er, nev-er use, What-ev-er the e-mer-gen-

Sorry Her Lot Who Loves Too Well

H.M.S. PINAFORE

Words by W.S. Gilbert
Music by Arthur Sullivan

hope _____ is dead!

Andante

Sad is the hour _____ when sets the sun— Dark is the

night _____ to earth's poor daugh - ters, When _____ to the ark _____ the

wea - ried one Flies from the emp - ty waste of wa - ters.

I Am the Monarch of the Sea

H.M.S. PINAFORE

Words by W.S. Gilbert
Music by Arthur Sullivan

when the breez - es blow   I gen-er-al-ly go be - low,   And   seek the se-clu-sion that a

HEBE:

ca - bin grants. And   so   do his sis - ters and his   cous-ins and his aunts, And   so   do his sis - ters and his

CHORUS:

cous - ins and his aunts And   so   do his sis - ters and his   cous - ins and his aunts,   His

sis - ters and his cous - ins, Whom he reck-ons up by doz-ens, and his   aunts.

When I Was a Lad

H.M.S. PINAFORE

Words by W.S. Gilbert
Music by Arthur Sullivan

tor - ney's firm, I I cleaned the win - dows and I
jun - ior clerk. I I served the writs with a a
soon be - came; I I wore clean col - lars and a
part - ner - ship, And that jun - ior part - ner -

swept the floor, And I pol - ished up the han - dle of the
smile so bland, And I cop - ied all the let - ters in a
bran' new suit, For the pass ex - am - i - na - tion at the
ship I ween, Was the on - ly ship____ that I

CHORUS:

big front door. He pol - ished up the han - dle of the
big round hand. He cop - ied all the let - ters in a
In - sti - tute. For the pass ex - am - i - na - tion at the
ev - er had seen. Was the on - ly ship____ he____

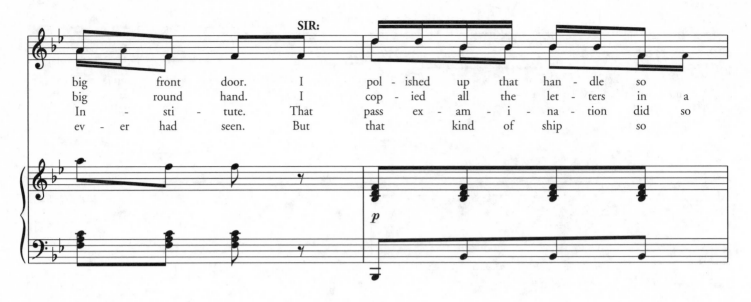

now he is the rul - er of the Queen's Na - vee.
now he is the rul - er of the Queen's Na - vee.
now he is the rul - er of the Queen's Na - vee.
now he is the rul - er of the Queen's Na - vee.

Queen's Na - vee.

5. I grew so rich that I was sent
   By a pocket borough into Parliament.
   I always voted at my party's call,
   And I never thought of thinking for myself at all.
   I thought so little they rewarded me,
   By making me the ruler of the Queen's Navee.

   CHORUS.— He thought so little, etc.

6. Now landsmen all, whoever you may be,
   If you want to rise to the top of the tree,
   If your soul isn't fettered to an office stool,
   Be careful to be guided by this golden rule,—
   Stick close to your desks and never go to sea,
   And you all may be rulers of the Queen's Navee.

   CHORUS.— Stick close, etc.

Refrain, Audacious Tar

H.M.S. PINAFORE

Words by W.S. Gilbert
Music by Arthur Sullivan

born Or I ___ more __ low - ly! I'd laugh my rank to scorn In un - ion

ho - ly, Were he more high - ly born Or I more low - ly!

Tempo I

RALPH: *f*

Proud

la - dy, have your way, Un - feel - ing __ beau - ty! You

speak, and I o - bey, It is __ my __ du - ty! I

am the low - liest tar that sails the wa - ter, And you, proud maid - en, are My

cap-tain's daugh - ter; Proud la - dy, have your way, You speak, and I o -

Un poco più lento

p (aside)

bey. My heart, with an-guish torn, Bows down __ be -

Fair Moon, to Thee I Sing

H.M.S. PINAFORE

Words by W.S. Gilbert
Music by Arthur Sullivan

real - ly pop - u - lar com-mand - er. But now my kind - ly crew re -

bel, _____ My daugh-ter to a tar is par - tial, Sir

Jo - seph storms, and, sad to tell, He threat - ens _____ a court -

cresc.

mar - tial! Fair moon, to thee _ I _ sing,

f   *p*

f   *dim.*   *pp*

Bright re - gent of the heav - ens, Say, why is ___

ev - 'ry - thing ___ Ei - ther at six - es or at sev - ens?

Fair moon, to thee I sing, ___ Bright ___ re - gent of the

heavens!

A Simple Sailor Lowly Born

H.M.S. PINAFORE

Words by W.S. Gilbert
Music by Arthur Sullivan

What I am giv - ing up, and whith - er go - ing.

On the one hand, papa's luxurious home,
Hung with ancestral armour and old brass - es,

Carved oak and tapestry from distant Rome,
Rare "blue and white," Venetian finger - glass - es,

Rich Oriental rugs,
luxurious sofa, pil - lows, And ev - 'ry - thing that is - n't old, from

Gil - lows!

And, on the other, a dark and dingy room
In some back street with stuffy children cry - ing,

Where organs yell, and clacking housewives
fume, And clothes are hanging out all day a - dry - ing,

With one cracked looking -
glass to see your face in,

And

dinner served up
in a pudding -

bas - in!

Allegro con spirito

cresc. molto

f

A sim - ple sail - or, low - ly born, Un -

let - tered and un - known, Who toils for bread from ear - ly morn Till

half the night has flown, Till half the night has flown! No gold-en rank can he im-part, No wealth of house or land, No for-tune, save his trust-y heart, And hon-est, brown right hand, his trust-y heart, and brown right hand! And yet he is so won-d'rous fair, That

love for one so pass - ing rare, So peer-less in his man - ly beau - ty, Were

lit - tle else than sol - emn du - ty, Were lit - tle else than sol - emn

rall. *ad lib.*

du - ty! Oh, god of love, and god of rea - son, say, ___ Which of you

rall. *p colla voce*

a tempo

twain shall my poor heart o - bey! A sim - ple sail - or, low - ly born, Un -

a tempo

let-tered and un-known. _____ No gold-en rank can he im-part, No wealth of house or land, No for-tune, save his trust-y heart, And hon-est, brown right hand, his trust-y heart and right hand! Oh, god of love, and god of rea-son, say, Which of you twain shall

my poor heart, ___ my poor heart o - bey, God of love,

god of rea - son, god of rea - son, god of love, say, ___

___ Which shall my poor heart o -

bey! Oh, god of love, and god of rea - son, say, Oh,

god of love, and god of rea - son, say, Which of you twain shall my poor

heart _____ o - bey, _____ my _____ heart _____ o -

heart _____ o -

opt.

bey, Which shall my heart, _____ my heart o -

bey!

bey!

He Is an Englishman!

H.M.S. PINAFORE

Words by W.S. Gilbert
Music by Arthur Sullivan

man! He re - mains __ an __ Eng - - - lish -

CHORUS:

a tempo

man! For in spite of all temp - ta - tions To be -

long to oth - er na - tions, He re - mains an Eng - lish -

man! He re - mains __ an __ Eng - - - lish - man!

When Frederic Was a Little Lad

THE PIRATES OF PENZANCE

Words by W.S. Gilbert
Music by Arthur Sullivan

RUTH:

1. When Fred - 'ric was a ___ lit - tle lad he ___
2. I was a stu - pid ___ nurs - 'ry - maid, on ___
3. I soon found out, be - yond all doubt, the ___

proved so brave and dar - ing, His fa - ther thought he'd ___
break - ers al - ways steer - ing, And I did not catch the ___
scope of this dis - as - ter, But I had - n't the face to re -

har - dy lad, though _ sure - ly not a high lot, Though
was to make, and _ doom him to a vile lot, I
find me now, a _ mem - ber of your shy lot, Which you

I'm a nurse, you might do worse than make your boy a a
bound him to a pi - rate— you!— in - stead of to a a
would -n't have found, had he been bound ap - pren - tice to a a

1, 2
pi - lot!
pi - lot!

3
pi - lot!

f f

I Am a Pirate King

THE PIRATES OF PENZANCE

Words by W.S. Gilbert
Music by Arthur Sullivan

Oh, Is There Not One Maiden Breast

THE PIRATES OF PENZANCE

Words by W.S. Gilbert
Music by Arthur Sullivan

* When performed as a solo with piano, a cut may be made to **.

seems to feel the mor - al beau - ty Of mak - ing world-ly in - ter - est Sub -

or - di - nate to sense of du - ty!

FREDERIC:

Oh,

is there not one maid-en here Whose home-ly face and bad com - plex - ion Have

caused all hope to dis - ap-pear Of ev - er win-ning man's af - fec - tion? To

such a one, If such there be, I swear, by heav-en's arch a - bove you, If

you will cast your eyes on me, How - ev - er plain you be, I'll love you, How -

rall. *a tempo* **ff**

ev - er plain you be, If you will cast your eyes on me, How - ev - er plain you be, I'll

a tempo

rall. *dolce* **pp** *cresc.*

love ____ you, I'll love ____ you, I'll love, ____ I'll love ____ you!

f **fz**

Poor Wand'ring One
THE PIRATES OF PENZANCE

Words by W.S. Gilbert
Music by Arthur Sullivan

heart ___ but ours! Take heart, fair days will shine; ___ Take

a - ny heart, take mine! Take heart,

no dan - ger lowers, Take _____ a - ny heart ___ but ours!

Take ___ heart, fair days will shine; ___ Take a - ny heart, take

Poor _____ wan - d'ring one! Ah, ah! _____ Ah, ah,

ah! Ah, ah! _____ Ah, ah, ah! Fair day will

shine, Take _____ heart! _____

Take _____ mine!   Take _____ heart! _____

_p_   _pp_

Take   mine!
Take

CHORUS:

_f_   _a tempo_

heart! no dan - ger lowers; Take a - ny

MABEL:

heart ____ but ours. Ah! ah! _____

Ah, _____ Take heart!

I Am the Very Model
of a Modern Major-General

THE PIRATES OF PENZANCE

Words by W.S. Gilbert
Music by Arthur Sullivan

MAJOR-GENERAL:

1. I
2. I

ver - y well ac - quaint - ed, too, with mat - ters math - e - mat - i - cal, I
tell un - doubt - ed Ra - pah - els from Ger - ard Dows and Zof - fa - nies, I

un - der - stand e - qua - tions, both the sim - ple and quad - rat - i - cal, A -
know the croak - ing cho - rus from the *Frogs* of Ar - is - toph - a - nes! Then

bout bi - no - mial the - o - rem I'm teem - ing with a lot o' news,
I can hum a fugue of which I've heard the mu - sic's din a - fore,

(Bothered for next rhyme— struck with an idea— joyfully)

With man - y cheer - ful facts a - bout the
And whis - tle all the airs from that in -

CHORUS:

square of the hy - pot - e - nuse. With many cheer - ful facts a - bout the
fer - nal non - sense, *Pin - a - fore!* And whis - tle all the airs from that in -

square of the hy - pot - e - nuse, With man - y cheer - ful facts a - bout the
fer - nal non - sense, *Pin - a - fore,* And whis - tle all the airs from that in -

square of the hy - pot - e - nuse, With many cheer - ful facts a - bout the
fer - nal non - sense, *Pin - a - fore,* And whis - tle all the airs from that in -

square of the hy - pot - e - pot - e - nuse.
fer - nal non - sense, *Pin - a - pin - a - fore.*

Slower

MG:

mod-ern Ma - jor - Gen - er - al.

3. In

pp

fact, when I know what is meant by "mam - e - lon" and "rav - e - lin", When I can tell at sight a Mau - ser

ri - fle from a jav - e - lin, When such af - fairs as sor - ties and sur - pris - es I'm more wa - ry at, And

when I know pre - cise - ly what is meant by "com - mis - sa - ri - at", When I have learnt what prog - ress has been

made in mod-ern gun-ner-y, When I know more of tac-tics than a

nov-ice in a nun-ner-y— In short, when I've a smat-ter-ing of

(Bothered for a rhyme— struck with an idea)

Vivace

el-e-men-tal strat-e-gy— You'll say a bet-ter Ma-jor-Gen-er-

CHORUS:

f

al has nev-er *sat* a gee You'll say a bet-ter Ma-jor-Gen-er-

f

al has nev - er *sat* a gee, You'll say a bet - ter Ma - jor-Gen - er - al has nev - er *sat* a gee, You'll

say a bet - ter Ma - jor - Gen - er - al has nev - er *sat* a, *sat* a gee.

fz

MG:

pp

4. For my mil - i - ta - ry know-ledge, tho' I'm pluck - y and ad - ven - tur - y, Has

on - ly been brought down to the be - gin - ning of the cen - tu - ry; But still, in mat - ters veg - e - ta - ble,

CHORUS:

an - i - mal, and min - er - al, I am the ver - y mod - el of a mod - ern Ma - jor - Gen - er - al. But

still, in mat - ters veg - e - ta - ble, an - i - mal, and min - er - al, He is the ver - y mod - el of a

mod - ern Ma - jor - Gen - er - al.

The Policeman's Song

THE PIRATES OF PENZANCE

Words by W.S. Gilbert
Music by Arthur Sullivan

Allegro moderato

SERGEANT: **CHORUS:** **SERGEANT:**

1. When a fel - on's not en - gaged in his em - ploy - ment, his em - ploy - ment, Or ma -
2. When the en - ter - pris - ing bur - glar's not a - bur - gling, not a - bur - gling, When the

CHORUS: **S:**

tur - ing his fe - lo - nious lit - tle plans, lit - tle plans, His ca -
cut - throat is - n't oc - cu - pied in crime, —pied in crime, He ____

With Cat-Like Tread,
Upon Our Prey We Steal

THE PIRATES OF PENZANCE

Words by W.S. Gilbert
Music by Arthur Sullivan

never speak a word; A fly's foot-fall Would be dis-tinct - ly heard— Ta-ran - ta-

ra, ta - ran - ta - ra! So stealth - i -

ly the pi - rate creeps, While all the house - hold sound - ly sleeps.

Come, friends, who plough the sea,

120

SAMUEL: *(distributing implements to various members*

of the gang)

Twenty Love-Sick Maidens We

PATIENCE

Words by W.S. Gilbert
Music by Arthur Sullivan

Twen - ty love-sick maid-ens we, _____ Love - sick all a-gainst our

will. _____ Twen - ty years hence we shall be

Twen - ty love - sick maid - ens still!

Twen - ty love - sick maid - ens we, And we die for love of

thee! Twen - ty love - sick maid - ens we, _____ Love - sick all a - gainst our

heart, go hide thy-self a - way, To weep - ing

con - cords tune thy roun - de - lay! Ah, mis - er - ie!

CHORUS:

All our love is all for one, Yet that love he heed - eth not, He is

coy and cares for none, Sad and sor - ry is our lot! Ah,

ELLA:

mis - er - ie! Go, break - ing heart, _____ Go, dream of love re - quit - ed! Go, fool - ish heart, _____ Go, dream of lov - ers

Twen - ty years hence we shall be

Twen - ty love - sick maid - ens still.

8va

Ah, mis - er -

ie!

mf *rall.* *p*

When I First Put This Uniform On

PATIENCE

Words by W.S. Gilbert
Music by Arthur Sullivan

COLONEL:

1. When I

first put this u - ni-form on, I said, as I looked in the glass, "It's
said, when I first put it on, "It is plain to the ver - i - est dunce, That

one to a mil - lion That an - y ci - vil - ian My fig - ure and form will sur - pass. Gold
ev - er - y beau - ty Will feel it her du - ty To yield to its glam - our at once. They will

lace has a charm for the fair, And I've plen - ty of that, and to spare, While a
see that I'm free - ly gold - laced In a u - ni - form hand - some and chaste"— But the

lov - er's pro - fes - sions, When ut - tered in Hes - sians, Are el - o - quent ev - 'ry - where! A
per - i - pa - tet - ics Of long - haired aes - thet - ics Are ver - y much more to their taste— Which

CHORUS:
f

fact that I count - ed up - on, When I first put this u - ni - form on! By a
I nev - er count - ed up - on, When I first put this u - ni - form on! By a

Am I Alone and Unobserved?
PATIENCE

Words by W.S. Gilbert
Music by Arthur Sullivan

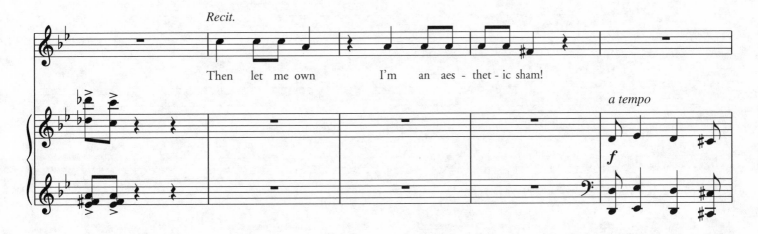

Let me con- fess! A

Recit.

languid love for lilies does *not* blight me! Lank limbs and haggard cheeks do *not* delight me! I do

not care for dirty greens By any means. I do *not* long for all one sees That's Japanese.— I am

not fond of uttering platitudes In stained-glass attitudes. In short, my

me-di-ae-val-is-m's af-fec-ta-tion, Born of a mor-bid love of ad-mi-ra-tion!

Allegretto grazioso ♩ = 76

1. If you're anx-ious for to shine — in the
el - o-quent in praise — of the
sen - ti-men-tal pas-sion of a

high aes - thet - ic line — as a man of cul - ture rare, You must
ver - y dull old days — which have long since passed a - way, And con -
veg - e - ta - ble fash - ion must ex - cite your lan - guid spleen, An at -

get up all the germs_ of the tran-scen-den-tal terms,_ and_ plant them ev-'ry-
vince 'em, if you can,_ that the reign of good Queen Anne_ was_ Cul-ture's palm-iest
tach-ment *à la* Pla-to for a bash-ful young po-ta-to, or a not-too-French French

where. You must lie up-on the dais-es and dis-course in nov-el phras-es of your
day. Of_ course_ you will pooh-pooh what ev-er's fresh and new,_ and de-
bean! Though the Phil-is-tines may jos-tle, you will rank as an a-pos-tle in the

com-pli-cat-ed state of mind, The mean-ing does-n't mat-ter if it's
clare it's crude and mean, For Art stopped short in the
high aes-thet-ic band, If you walk down Pic-ca-dil-ly with a

on-ly i-dle chat-ter of a tran-scen-den-tal
cul-ti-vat-ed court of the Em-press Jo-seph-
pop-py or a lil-y in your me-di-ae-val

last verse rall.

terms too deep for *me,* Why,
good e - nough for *me,* Why,
cer - tain - ly not suit *me,* Why,

what a ver - y sin - gu - lar - ly deep young man this
what a ver - y cul - ti - va - ted kind of youth this
what a most par - tic - u - lar - ly pure young man this

last verse rall.

deep young man must be!"
kind of youth must be!"
pure young youth man must be!"

2. Be
3. Then a

Prithee, Pretty Maiden

PATIENCE

Words by W.S. Gilbert
Music by Arthur Sullivan

PATIENCE:

Silver'd Is the Raven Hair

PATIENCE

Words by W.S. Gilbert
Music by Arthur Sullivan

Recit. **JANE:**

Sad is that wom-an's lot who, year by year,

Sees, one by one, her beau-ties dis - ap-pear:

When Time, grown wea-ry of her heart-drawn sighs, Im-pa-tient-ly be-gins to dim her

eyes! Com-pelled at last, in

life's un-cer-tain gloam-ings, To

wreathe her wrin-kled brow with well-saved "comb-ings," Re -

shape - ly — limb, And al-though se - vere-ly — laced, Spread-ing is the — fig - ure trim!

rall.   *a tempo*

Stout - er than I used to be, Still more cor-pu - lent grow I— There will be too

rall.   *p a tempo*

appassionato

f   *ff*

much — of — me In the com - ing by and bye! There will be too much of me In the

mf

com - ing — by and bye!

[*colla voce*]   *a tempo*   *f*

Love Is a Plaintive Song

PATIENCE

Words by W.S. Gilbert
Music by Arthur Sullivan

The Law Is the True Embodiment

IOLANTHE

Words by W.S. Gilbert
Music by Arthur Sullivan

Allegro vivace

LORD CHANCELLOR:

1. The Law is the true em-bod-i-ment Of ev-'ry-thing that's
2. But though the com-pli-ment im-plied In-flates me with le-
3. And ev-'ry-one who'd mar-ry a Ward must come to me for

ex-cel-lent. It has no kind of fault or flaw, And
git-i-mate pride, It nev-er-the-less can't be de-nied That it
my ac-cord, And in my court I sit all day,

When I Went to the Bar
as a Very Young Man

IOLANTHE

Words by W.S. Gilbert
Music by Arthur Sullivan

LORD CHANCELLOR:

1. When I
2. Ere I
3. I'll
4. In

went	to	the	Bar	as	a	ver	y	young man	(Said
go	in	to	court	I	will	read	my	brief through	(Said
nev	er	throw	dust	in	a	ju	ry	man's eyes	(Said
oth	er	pro	fes	sions	in	which	men	en gage	(Said

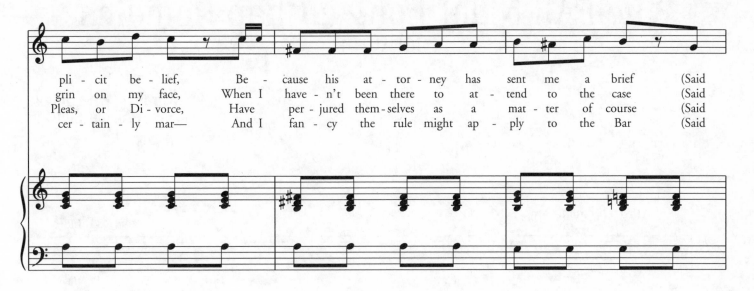

pli – cit be – lief,   Be – cause his at – tor – ney has sent me a brief   (Said
grin on my face,   When I have – n't been there to at – tend to the case   (Said
Pleas, or Di – vorce,   Have per – jured them – selves as a mat – ter of course   (Said
cer – tain – ly mar—   And I fan – cy the rule might ap – ply to the Bar   (Said

I to my – self— said I).
I to my – self— said I).
I to my – self— said I).
I to my – self— said I)!

When All Night Long a Chap Remains

IOLANTHE

Words by W.S. Gilbert
Music by Arthur Sullivan

is,   as - sum - ing that he's got an - y.   Tho' nev - er nur - tured
vote   just as their lead - ers tell 'em to.   But then the pros - pect

in the lap Of lux - u - ry,   yet I ad - mon - ish you,   I
of a lot Of dull M. P.'s   in close prox - im - i - ty,   All

am an in - tel - lec - tual chap, And think of things that would as -
think - ing for them - selves, is what No man can face with e - qua -

Tempo primo ♩ = 69

ton - ish you.   I of - ten think it's com - i - cal—
nim - i - ty.   Then let's re - joice with loud Fal, lal—

p

Fal, lal, _____ la! Fal, lal, _____ la! How {
Fal, lal, _____ la! Fal, lal, _____ la! That { Na - ture al - ways

does con - trive— Fal, lal, _____ la, _____ la! That _____

ev - 'ry boy and _____ ev - 'ry gal That's born in - to the _____

world a - live Is ei - ther a lit - tle Lib - er - al Or

poco rit.

poco rit.

else a lit - tle Con - serv - a - tive! Fal, lal, ___ la!

Fal, lal, ___ la! Is ei - ther a lit - tle Lib - er - al Or

else a lit - tle Con - serv - a - tive! Fal, lal, la!

2. When

When Britain Really Ruled the Waves

IOLANTHE

Words by W.S. Gilbert
Music by Arthur Sullivan

em - i - nence, Or schol - ar - ship sub - lime; Yet Brit - ain won her
ti - cu - lar, And did it ver - y well: Yet Brit - ain set the
mat - ters which They do not un - der - stand, As bright will shine Great

proud - est bays In good Queen Bess - 's glo - rious days! Yet Brit - ain won her
world a - blaze In good King George - 's glo - rious days! Yet Brit - ain set the
Brit - ain's rays As in King George - 's glo - rious days! As bright will shine Great

f **CHORUS:** *più lento*

proud - est bays In good Queen Bess - 's glo - rious days. Yes, Brit - ain won her
world a - blaze In good King George - 's glo - rious days. Yes, Brit - ain set the
Brit - ain's rays As in King George - 's glo - rious days. As bright will shine Great

ff *più lento*

1, 2 **LORD M:** **3**

proud - est bays In good Queen Bess - 's glo - rious days. When
world a - blaze In good King George - 's glo - rious days. And
Brit - ain's rays As in King George - 's glo - rious days.

Oh, Foolish Fay

IOLANTHE

Words by W.S. Gilbert
Music by Arthur Sullivan

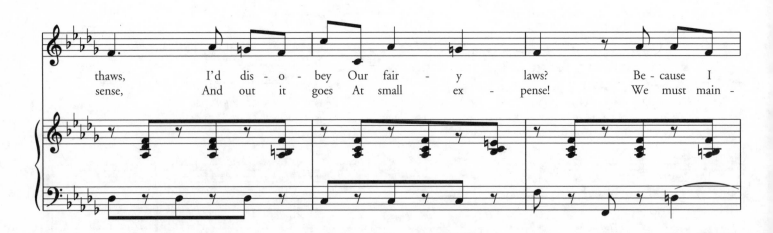

Love, Unrequited, Robs Me of My Rest

IOLANTHE

Words by W.S. Gilbert
Music by Arthur Sullivan

Love, night-mare-like, lies heav-y on my chest, And

a tempo

weaves it-self in-to my mid-night slum - bers!

p

fz

Allegro ma non troppo ♩. = 100

When you're

ly - ing a - wake with a dis - mal head - ache, and re - pose is ta - boo'd by anx - i - e - ty, I con -

ceive you may use an - y lan - guage you choose to in - dulge in, with - out im - pro - pri - e - ty; For your

brain is on fire __ the bed - clothes con - spire __ of u - su - al slum - ber to plun - der you: First your

coun - ter - pane goes, and un - cov - ers your toes, and your sheet slips de - mure - ly from un - der you; Then the

blank-et-ing tick-les— you feel like mixed pick-les— so ter-ri-bly sharp is the prick-ing, And you're

hot, and you're cross, and you tum-ble and toss till there's noth-ing 'twixt you and the tick-ing. Then the

bed-clothes all creep to the ground in a heap, and you pick 'em all up in a tan-gle; Next your

pil-low re-signs and po-lite-ly de-clines to re-main at its u-su-al an-gle! Well, you

driv-ing like mad with this sin-gu-lar lad (by-the-bye, the ship's now a four-wheel-er), And you're

play-ing round games, and he calls you bad names when you tell him that "ties pay the deal-er"; But

this you can't stand, so you throw up your hand, and you find you're as cold as an i-ci-cle; In your

shirt and your socks (the black silk with gold clocks), cross-ing Sal's-bu-ry Plain on a bi-cy-cle: And

a piacere

dit - to my song—

And thank good - ness they're

f colla voce

(Lord Chancellor falls exhausted on a seat.)

both of them o - ver!

Con fuoco

ff

If You Give Me Your Attention

PRINCESS IDA

Words by W.S. Gilbert
Music by Arthur Sullivan

Allegro non troppo

KING GAMA:

1. If you give me your at - ten - tion, I will tell you what I am: I'm a gen - u - ine phi - lan - thro - pist, all
2. To com - pli - ments in - flat - ed I've a with - er - ing re - ply, And van - i - ty I al - ways do my
3. I'm sure I'm no as - cet - ic; I'm as pleas - ant as can be; You'll al - ways find me read - y with a

oth - er kinds are sham. Each lit - tle fault of tem - per and each
best to mor - ti - fy; A char - i - ta - ble action I can
crush - ing rep - ar - tee. I've an ir - ri - tat - ing chuck - le, I've a

so - ci - al de - fect In my err - ing fel - low crea - tures, I en -
skil - ful - ly dis - sect; And in - ter - est - ed mo - tives I'm de -
cel - e - brat - ed sneer, I've an en - ter - tain - ing snig - ger, I've a

deav - our to cor - rect. To all their lit - tle weak - ness - es I o - pen peo - ple's eyes; And
light - ed to de - tect. I know ev - 'ry - bod - y's in - come and what ev - 'ry - bod - y earns; And I
fas - ci - nat - ing leer. To ev - 'ry - bod - y's prej - u - dice I know a thing or two; I can

lit - tle plans to snub the self - suf - fi - cient I de - vise; I
care - ful - ly com - pare it with the in - come tax re - turns; But to
tell a wom - an's age in half a min - ute, and I do. But al -

Oh, Goddess Wise

PRINCESS IDA

Words by W.S. Gilbert
Music by Arthur Sullivan

fer - vent few Have come to woo The rays that from thee fall, _____

_____ that from thee fall. Oh, god - dess wise That

lov - est _____ light, _____ That lov - est light, _____

Let fer - vent words and fer - vent thoughts be mine, _____ That

I may — lead them to thy sa-cred shrine!

Let fer - vent words and fer - vent thoughts be mine, That I ____

_____ may lead them to thy sa - cred _ shrine _ I ___ may ___ lead them to thy

cresc. molto

ff

sa - cred shrine, thy sa - cred shrine!

A Wand'ring Minstrel I

THE MIKADO

Words by W.S. Gilbert
Music by Arthur Sullivan

sor - row! On maid-en's cold-ness do you brood? I'll do so, too—

Oh, _____ sor - row, _ sor - row! I'll charm your will - ing

ears with songs of lov-ers' fears, While sym-pa-thet-ic

tears __ My cheeks be-dew __ Oh, _____ sor - row, _ sor - row!

sail - or ___ sees Is when he's down At an in - land ___ town, With his Nan - cy on his

CHORUS:

knees, yeo - ho! And his arm ___ a - round her waist! Then man the cap - stan—

off we go, As the fid - dler swings us round, With a

yeo heave - ho, And a rum ___ be - low, Hur - rah for the home - ward

bound! _____ With a yeo heave - ho, _____ And a

Yeo - ho, heave -

rum be - low, _____ Yeo - ho, heave - ho, _____

ho, Yeo - ho,

Yeo - ho, _____ heave - ho, heave - ho, heave - ho, yeo -

ho!

As Some Day It May Happen

THE MIKADO

Words by W.S. Gilbert
Music by Arthur Sullivan

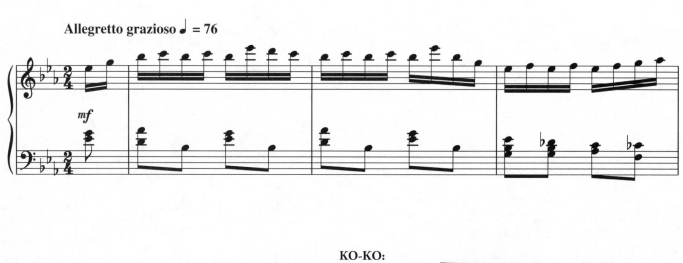

Allegretto grazioso ♩ = 76

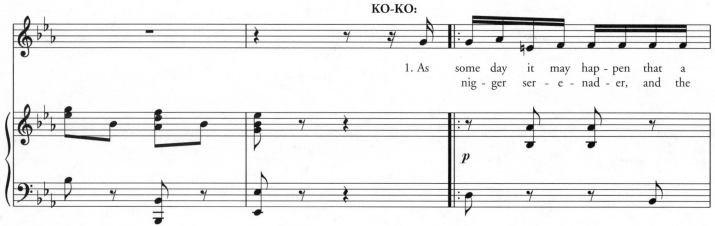

KO-KO:

1. As some day it may hap-pen that a
   nig - ger ser - e - nad - er, and the

vic - tim must be found, I've got a lit - tle list— I've got a lit - tle list of so -
oth - ers of his race, And the pia - no - or - gan - ist— I've got him on the list! And the

ci - e - ty of - fend - ers who might well be un - der-ground, And who nev - er would be missed— who

peo - ple who eat pep - per - mint and puff it in your face, They nev - er would be missed— they

nev - er would be missed! There's the pes - ti - len - tial nui - san - ces who write for au - to-graphs— All

nev - er would be missed! Then the id - i - ot who prais - es, with en - thu - si - as - tic tone, All

peo - ple who have flab - by hands and ir - ra - tat - ing laughs— All chil - dren who are up in dates, and

cen - tu - ries but this, and ev - 'ry coun - try but his own; And the la - dy from the prov - in - ces, who

floor you with 'em flat— All per - sons who in shak - ing hands, shake hands with you like *that*— And

dress - es like a guy, And "who does - n't think she danc - es, but would rath - er like to try"; And that

all third per-sons who on spoil-ing *tête - à - têtes* in - sist— They'd none of 'em be missed— they'd
sin - gu - lar a - nom - a - ly, the la - dy nov - el - ist— I don't think she'd be missed— I'm

CHORUS:

none of 'em be missed! He's got 'em on the list— he's got 'em on the list; And they'll
sure she'd not be missed! He's got her on the list— he's got her on the list; And I

1 **KO-KO:** 2 **KO-KO:**

none of 'em be missed— they'll none of 'em be missed! 2. There's the
don't think she'll be missed— I'm *sure* she'll not be missed! 3. And that

Ni - si Pri - us nui-sance, who just now is rath - er rife, The ju - di - cial hu - mor - ist— I've

got *him* on the list! All fun-ny fel-lows, com-ic men, and clowns of pri-vate life— They'd

none of 'em be missed— they'd none of 'em be missed! And a-pol-o-get-ic states-men of a

com-pro-mis-ing kind, Such as— What d'ye call him— Thing-'em-bob, and like-wise— Nev-er mind, And

colla voce

St— st— st— and What's-his-name, and al-so You-know-who— The task of fill-ing up the blanks I'd

rath - er leave to *you.* But it real - ly does - n't mat - ter whom you

CHORUS:

put up - on the list, For they'd none of 'em be missed— they'd none of 'em be missed! You may

put 'em on the list— you may put 'em on the list; And they'll none of 'em be missed— they'll

none of 'em be missed!

Three Little Maids from School Are We

THE MIKADO

Words by W.S. Gilbert
Music by Arthur Sullivan

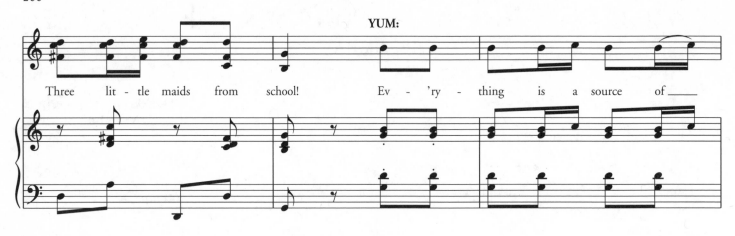

YUM:

Three lit - tle maids from school! Ev - 'ry - thing is a source of ____

fun. *(Chuckle)*

PEEP:

No - bod - y's

safe, for we care for ___ none! *(Chuckle)*

PITTI:

Life is a joke that's ___ just be - gun! *(Chuckle)*

YUM, PEEP, PITTI:

202

The Sun, Whose Rays Are All Ablaze

THE MIKADO

Words by W.S. Gilbert
Music by Arthur Sullivan

YUM-YUM:

1. The sun, whose rays Are all a - blaze With ev - er - liv - ing glo - ry,
2. Ob - serve his flame, That plac - id dame, The moons Ce - les - tial High - ness;

Does not de - ny His maj - es - ty— He scorns to tell a sto - ry!
There's not a trace Up - on her face Of dif - fi - dence or shy - ness:

He won't ex-claim, "I blush for shame, So kind-ly be in-dul-gent;"
She bor-rows light That, thro' the night, Man-kind may all ac-claim her!

But, fierce and bold, In fier-y gold, He glo-ries all ef-ful-gent.
And, truth to tell, She lights up well, So I, for one, don't blame her.

I mean to rule the earth, _____
Ah, pray make no mis-take, _____

Miya Sama

THE MIKADO

Words by W.S. Gilbert
Music by Arthur Sullivan

CHORUS:

Mi - ya sa - ma, mi - ya sa - ma, On n'm - ma no ma - yé ni Pi - ra Pi - ra su - ru no wa

Nan — gia — na — To - ko ton - ya - ré ton - ya - ré na!

Mi - ya sa - ma, mi - ya sa - ma, On n'm - ma no ma - yé ni Pi - ra Pi - ra su - ru no wa

Nan___ gia___ na_____ To - ko ton - ya - ré ton - ya - ré na!

MIKADO:

From ev - 'ry kind of man O - be - dience

KATISHA:

I___ ex - pect; I'm the Em-p'ror of Ja - pan— And I'm his daugh - ter-in - law e - lect! He'll

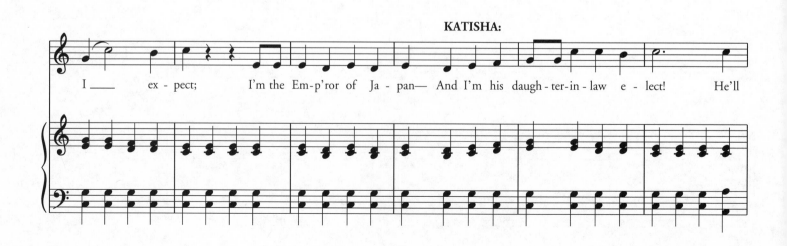

MIKADO:

mar-ry his son (He's on-ly got one) To his daugh-ter-in-law e-lect. My _ mor-als have been de-

KATISHA:

clared Par-tic-u-lar-ly cor-rect; But they're noth-ing at all, com-pared With those of his

daugh-ter-in-law e-lect. Bow— Bow— To his daugh-ter-in-law e-lect.

CHORUS:

_f_

Bow— Bow— To his daugh-ter-in-law e-lect.

dim.

212

213

The Mikado's Song

THE MIKADO

Words by W.S. Gilbert
Music by Arthur Sullivan

make each pris – 'ner pent   Un – will – ing – ly rep – re – sent   A

source   of in – no – cent mer – ri – ment,   Of in – no – cent mer – ri – ment!

All

pros – y dull   so – ci – e – ty sin – ners, Who   chat – ter and bleat   and

ad – ver – tis – ing quack   who wea – ries With   tales   of count – less

bore, _____ Are sent to hear ser-mons From mys-ti-cal Ger-mans Who
cures, _____ His teeth, I've en-act-ed, Shall all be ex-tract-ed By

preach from ten till four. The am-a-teur ten-or, whose vo-cal vil-lain-ies
ter-ri-fied am - a-teurs. The mu-sic-hall sing-er at-tends a se-ries Of

All de-sire ___ to shirk, Shall, dur-ing off-hours, _ Ex-hib-it his pow-ers To
mass-es and fugues _ and "ops" By Bach, in-ter-wov-en With Spohr and Bee-tho-ven, At

Mad-ame Tus-saud's _ wax-work. The la-dy who dyes a chem-i-cal yel-low, Or
clas-si-cal Mon - day Pops. The bil-liard sharp whom an-y-one catch-es, His

218

shall a-chieve in time— To let the pun-ish-ment fit the crime, The

pun-ish-ment fit the crime; And make each pris-'ner pent Un -

will-ing-ly rep - re - sent A source of in-no-cent mer - ri-ment, Of

CHORUS:

in-no-cent mer - ri - ment! His ob - ject all sub - lime He

The Flowers That Bloom in the Spring

THE MIKADO

Words by W.S. Gilbert
Music by Arthur Sullivan

ENSEMBLE:

flow - ers that bloom in the spring. Tra la la la la,___ Tra la la la la,___

Tra la la la la la!

KO-KO:

The flow - ers that bloom in the

spring, Tra la, Have noth - ing to do with the case. I've

ENSEMBLE: *f*

la   la la la, ___ Tra la   la la la, ___ "Oh, both - er the flow - ers of spring!"   Tra

la   la la la, ___ Tra la   la la la, ___   Tra   la la la   la   la! _____

Alone, and Yet Alive
THE MIKADO

Words by W.S. Gilbert
Music by Arthur Sullivan

KATISHA:

pris - on - er!

Re - mote the peace that Death a - lone can give—

My doom, to wait!

My pun - ish-ment, to live!

Andante moderato ♩ = 84

Hearts do not break!

They sting and ache For old — love's sake, But do not die,

Tho' with each breath They long for _ death, As wit - ness - eth The liv - ing

I, The liv - ing I. _____ Oh, liv - ing

I! Come, tell ____ me ____ why, When

hope is gone, Dost thou stay on? Why lin - ger here, Where

all   is   drear?   Oh,   liv -   ing

I!   Come, tell ___ me ___ why,   When   hope ____ is gone, Dost

thou   stay on?   May not   a   cheat - ed maid - en   die?   May   not ____

____ a   cheat - ed maid – en   die?

Willow, Tit-Willow
THE MIKADO

Words by W.S. Gilbert
Music by Arthur Sullivan

There Is Beauty in the Bellow of the Blast

THE MIKADO

Words by W.S. Gilbert
Music by Arthur Sullivan

li - on is a-roar - ing, And the ti - ger is a-lash - ing of his tail. **KK:** Yes, I
sub - ject in - ter-est - ing: Is a maid - en all the bet - ter when she's tough? **Ka:** Through -

like to see a ti - ger From the Con - go or the Ni - ger, And es -
out this wide do-min - ion It's the gen - er - al o - pin - ion That she'll

pe - cial-ly when lash - ing of his tail. **Ka:** Vol - ca - noes have a splen - dour that is
last a good deal long - er when she's tough. **KK:** Are you old e - nough to mar - ry, do you

grim, And earth - quakes on - ly ter - ri - fy the dolts, But to
think? Won't you wait un - til you're eight - y in the shade? There's a

tastes are one. A - way we'll go, And mer - ri - ly mar - ry, Nor tar - di - ly tar - ry Till
tastes are one. A - way we'll go, And mer - ri - ly mar - ry, Nor tar - di - ly tar - ry Till

day is done.

day is done. If that is so, Sing der - ry down der - ry! It's

ev – i – dent, ver – y, Our tastes are one. A – way we'll go, And mer – ri – ly mar – ry, Nor

tar – di – ly tar – ry Till day is done. Sing der – ry down der – ry! We'll mer – ri – ly mar – ry, Nor

tar – di – ly tar – ry Till day is done.

If Somebody There Chanced to Be

RUDDIGORE

Words by W.S. Gilbert
Music by Arthur Sullivan

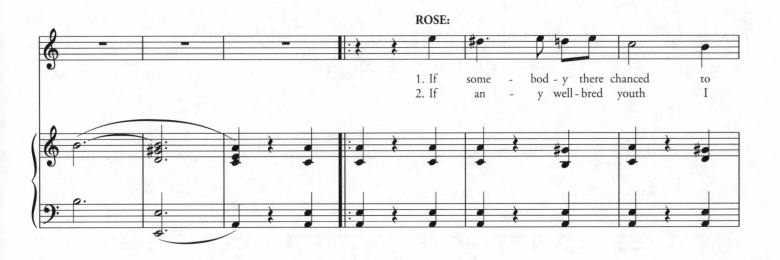

ROSE:

1. If some - bod - y there chanced to
2. If an - y well - bred youth I

be   Who loved   me in a   man - ner true,   My
knew,   Po - lite   and gen - tle, neat   and   trim,   Then

238

(searching book)

met, Is con - tra - ry to et - i - quette; Where can it
do To speak un - til you're spo - ken to. Where can it

(finding reference)

be? Now let me see— Yes, yes!
be? Now let me see— Yes, yes!

It's con - tra - ry to et - i - quette!
"Don't speak un - til you're spo - ken to!"

p

1

2

f *ff*

My Boy, You May Take It from Me

RUDDIGORE

Words by W.S. Gilbert
Music by Arthur Sullivan

worst.
gain.
place.

Though clev- er as clev- er can be—
I've a high- ly in- tel- li- gent face—
Then I sing and I play and I paint:

A
My
Though

Crich- ton of ear- ly ro- mance—
fea- tures can- not be de- nied—
none are ac- com- plished as I,

You must stir it and stump it, And
But, what- ev- er I try, sir, I
To say so were trea- son: You

(2nd & 3rd Verses)

blow your own trum- pet, Or, trust me, you have- n't a chance!
fail in— and why, sir? I'm mod- es- ty per- son- i- fied!
ask me the rea- son? I'm dif- fi- dent, mod- est, and shy!

p

If you wish in the world to ad- vance,

Your ___

pp

mer - its you're bound to en - hance, You must stir it and stump it, And

blow your own trum-pet, Or, trust me, you have - n't a chance! chance! If you

wish in the world to ad - vance, Your ____ mer - its you're bound to en - hance, You must

stir it and stump it, And blow your own trum-pet, Or, trust me, you have - n't a chance!

To a Garden Full of Posies

RUDDIGORE

Words by W.S. Gilbert
Music by Arthur Sullivan

Henceforth All the Crimes

RUDDIGORE

Words by W.S. Gilbert
Music by Arthur Sullivan

Allegro risoluto

ROBIN:

A-way, Re-morse! Com-punc-tion,

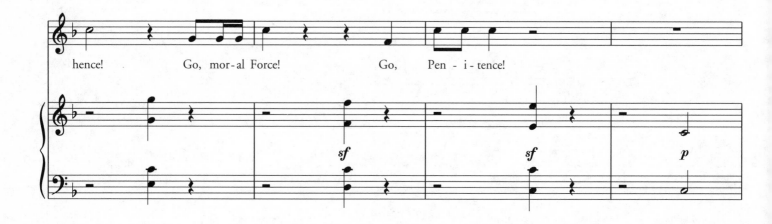

hence! Go, mor-al Force! Go, Pen-i-tence!

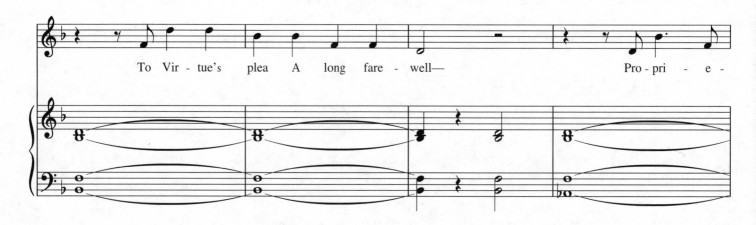

To Vir-tue's plea A long fare-well— Pro-pri-e-

ty, I ring your knell! Come, guilt-i-ness of dead-liest

hue! Come, des-p'rate deeds ___ of der-ring-do!

Allegro comodo ♩. = 120

1. Hence -
2. Ye
3. Ye

1. forth all the crimes that I find in the *Times* I've prom-ised to per-pe-trate
2. well - to - do squires, who live in the shires, Where pet - ty dis - tinc - tions are
3. sup - ple M. P.s', who go down on your knees, Your pre - cious i - den - ti - ty

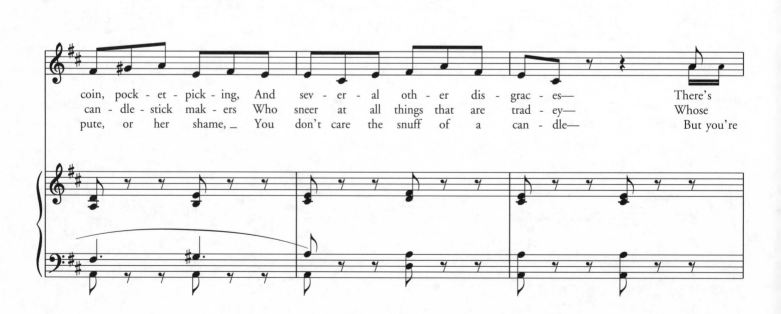

248

pos - tage-stamp prig - ging, and then, thim - ble - rig - ging, The three - card de - lu - sion at
mid - dle - class lives are em - bar - rassed by wives __ Who long to pa - rade as "My
paid for your game when you're told that your name Will be graced by a bar - on - et's

rac - es! Oh! _____ a bar - o - net's rank is ex -
La - dy," Oh! _____ al - low me to of - fer a
han - dle— Oh! _____ al - low me to give *you* a

ceed - ing - ly nice, But the ti - tle's un - com - mon - ly dear at the price!
word of ad - vice, The ti - tle's un - com - mon - ly dear at the price!
word of ad - vice— The ti - tle's un - com - mon - ly dear at the price!

f

When Maiden Loves, She Sits and Sighs

THE YEOMEN OF THE GUARD

Words by W.S. Gilbert
Music by Arthur Sullivan

1. When maid - en loves, she sits and sighs, She wan - ders to and fro; Un - bid - den tear-drops fill her eyes, And to all ques - tions she re - plies With a sad "Heigh - ho!"

2. When maid - en loves, she mopes a - part, As owl mopes on a tree; Al - though she keen - ly feels the smart, She can - not tell what ails her heart, With its

Is Life a Boon?

THE YEOMEN OF THE GUARD

Words by W.S. Gilbert
Music by Arthur Sullivan

2. Is life a thorn? Then count it not a whit! Nay, count it not a whit! Man is well done _____ with it; Soon _____ as he's born He should all means es- say To put the plague a - way; And I, war -

I Have a Song to Sing, O!

THE YEOMEN OF THE GUARD

Words by W.S. Gilbert
Music by Arthur Sullivan

sipped no sup, and he craved no crumb, As he sighed for the love of a la - dye!

ELSIE:

I have a song to sing, O!

POINT:

What is your song, O? _____ **ELSIE:** It is

sung with the ring Of the songs maids _ sing Who love with a love life - long, O! It's the

song of a mer-ry-maid, peer-ly proud, Who loved a lord, and who laughed a-loud At the

moan of the mer-ry-man, mop-ing mum, Whose soul was sad, and whose glance was glum, Who

sipped, no sup, and who craved no crumb, As he sighed for the love of a la - dye!

Heigh - dy! heigh - dy! Mis-er-y me, lack-a-day-dee! He

Heigh - dy! Heigh - dy! Mis - er - y me, lack - a - day - dee! His

pains were o'er, and he sighed no more, For he lived in the love of a la - dye! _____

I've Jibe and Joke

THE YEOMEN OF THE GUARD

Words by W.S. Gilbert
Music by Arthur Sullivan

I ply my craft And know no fear, But aim my shaft At prince or peer. At peer or prince— at prince or peer, I aim my shaft and know no fear!

rall.

trick you in-to learn-ing with a laugh; Oh, win-now all my fol-ly, fol-ly,
pleas-ant truths are swal-lowed with a will, For he who'd make his fel-low, fel-low,

sfz

fol-ly, and you'll find A grain or two of truth a-mong the chaff! Oh,
fel-low crea-tures wise Should al-ways gild the phil-o-soph-ic pill! For

sfz

win-now all my fol-ly, fol-ly, fol-ly, and you'll find A grain or two of truth a-mong the
he who'd make his fel-low, fel-low, fel-low crea-tures wise Should al-ways gild the phil-o-soph-ic

chaff!
pill!

2. I can

f

p

Were I Thy Bride

THE YEOMEN OF THE GUARD

Words by W.S. Gilbert
Music by Arthur Sullivan

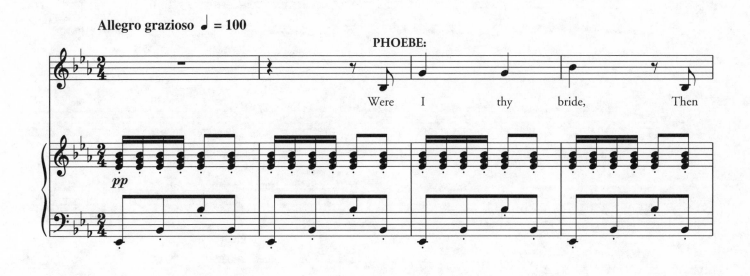

Were I thy bride! And all day long Our lives should be a song: No grief, no wrong Should make my heart re - bel— Were I thy bride! The sil - v'ry flute, The

Oh! A Private Buffoon
Is a Light-Hearted Loon

THE YEOMEN OF THE GUARD

Words by W.S. Gilbert
Music by Arthur Sullivan

Allegretto comodo ♩. = 112

POINT:

1. Oh! a pri - vate buf - foon is a light - heart - ed loon, If you
2. If you wish to suc - ceed as a jest - er, you'll need To con -
3. If your mas - ter is sur - ly, from get - ting up ear - ly (And
4. Comes a Bish - op, may - be, or a sol - emn D. D.— Oh, be -
5. Though your head it may rack with a bil - ious at - tack, And your

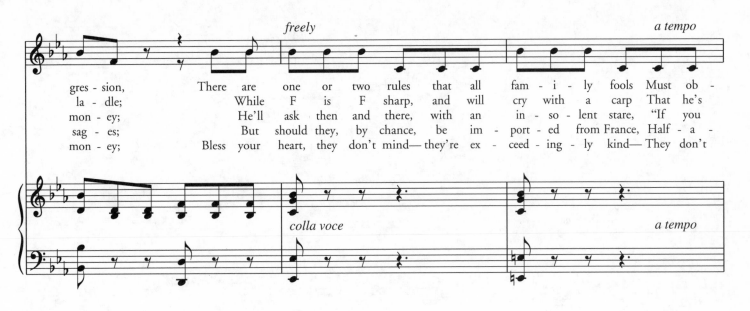

freely   *a tempo*

gres - sion,   There are one or two rules that all fam - i - ly fools Must ob -
la - dle;   While F is F sharp, and will cry with a carp That he's
mon - ey;   He'll ask then and there, with an in - so - lent stare, "If you
sag - es;   But should they, by chance, be im - port - ed from France, Half - a -
mon - ey;   Bless your heart, they don't mind—they're ex - ceed - ing - ly kind— They don't

colla voce   *a tempo*

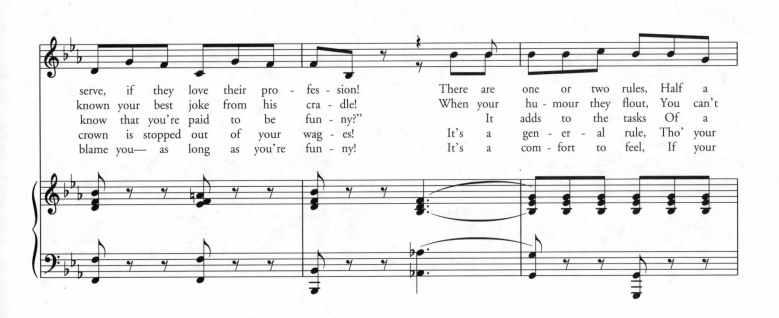

serve, if they love their pro - fes - sion!   There are one or two rules, Half a
known your best joke from his cra - dle!   When your hu - mour they flout, You can't
know that you're paid to be fun - ny?"   It adds to the tasks Of a
crown is stopped out of your wag - es!   It's a gen - er - al rule, Tho' your
blame you— as long as you're fun - ny!   It's a com - fort to feel, If your

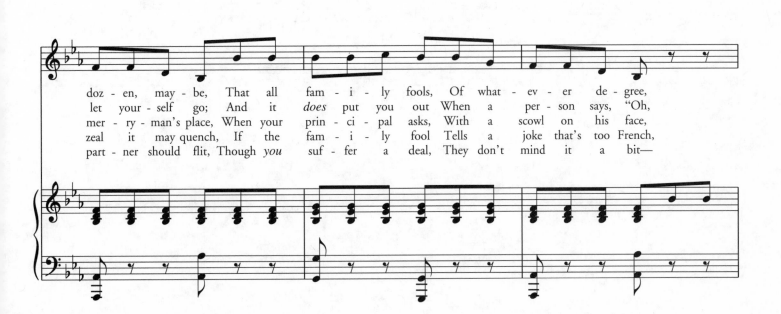

doz - en, may - be, That all fam - i - ly fools, Of what - ev - er de - gree,
let your - self go; And it *does* put you out When a per - son says, "Oh,
mer - ry - man's place, When your prin - ci - pal asks, With a scowl on his face,
zeal it may quench, If the fam - i - ly fool Tells a joke that's too French,
part - ner should flit, Though *you* suf - fer a deal, They don't mind it a bit—

Must ob - serve, if they love their pro - fes - sion.
I have known that old joke from my cra - dle!
If you know that you're paid to be fun - ny?
Half - a - crown is stopped out of his wag - es!
They don't blame you— so long as you're

fun - ny!

Free from His Fetters Grim

THE YEOMEN OF THE GUARD

Words by W.S. Gilbert
Music by Arthur Sullivan

Andante con espressione ♩ = 88

FAIRFAX:

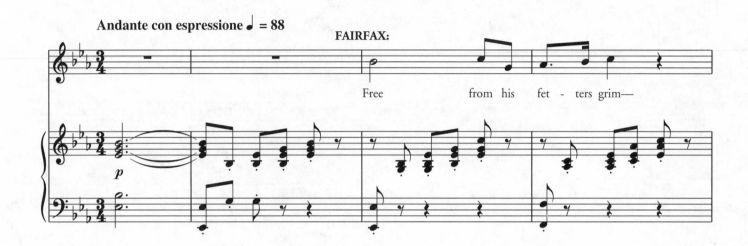

Free from his fet - ters grim—

Free to de - part;____ Free both in life and limb—

In all __ but __ heart! Bound to an un - known bride

For good and ill; Ah, is not one so tied _____ A

rit.

pris - 'ner _____ still, A pris - 'ner _____ still? *freely* Ah, is not one so

dim. *p*

a tempo

tied _____ A pris - 'ner still?

f a tempo

Free, yet in fet - ters held Till his last hour, _____ Gyves that no

smith can weld, No rust __ de - vour! Al - though a mon - arch's hand

Had set him free, Of all the cap - tive band __ The sad - dest

he, The sad - dest he! Of all the cap - tive band __ The

sad - dest, sad - dest he!

The Duke of Plaza-Toro

THE GONDOLIERS

Words by W.S. Gilbert
Music by Arthur Sullivan

Allegro marziale

DUKE:

1. In ___ en - ter - prise of ___ mar - tial kind, When there was a - ny ___
2. When, ___ to e - vade De - struc - tion's hand, To hide they all ___ pro -
3. When ___ told that they would ___ all be shot Un - less they left ___ the ___

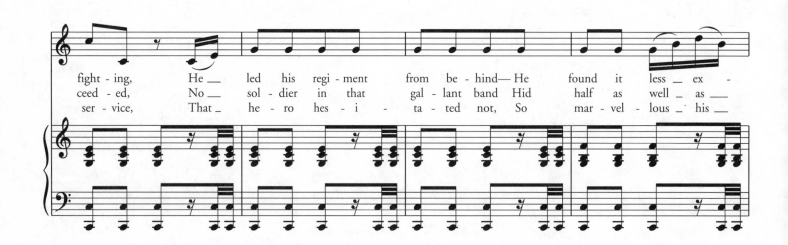

fight - ing, He ___ led his regi - ment from be - hind— He found it less ___ ex -
ceed - ed, No ___ sol - dier in that gal - lant band Hid half as well ___ as ___
ser - vice, That ___ he - ro hes - i - ta - ted not, So mar - vel - lous ___ his ___

cit - ing. But __ when a - way his regi - ment ran, His place was __ at the
he did. He __ lay con - ceal'd through - out the war, And so pre - serv'd his
nerve is. He __ sent his re - sig - na - tion in, The first of __ all his

fore, O! That cel - e - bra - ted, Cul - ti - va - ted, Un - der - ra - ted No - ble - man, The
gore, O! That un - af - fec - ted, Un - de - tec - ted, Well - con - nec - ted War - ri - or, The
corps, O! That ve - ry know - ing, O - ver - flow - ing, Ea - sy - go - ing Pa - la - din, The

ENSEMBLE:

Duke of Pla - za - To - ro! In the first and fore - most flight, ha, ha! You
Duke of Pla - za - To - ro! In ev - 'ry dough - ty deed, ha ha! He
Duke of Pla - za - To - ro! To men of gross - er clay, ha, ha! He

al - ways found that knight, ha, ha! That cel - e - bra - ted, Cul - ti - va - ted,
al - ways took the lead, ha, ha! That un - af - fec - ted, Un - de - tec - ted,
al - ways showed the way, ha, ha! That ve - ry know - ing, O - ver - flow - ing,

No Possible Doubt Whatever

THE GONDOLIERS

Words by W.S. Gilbert
Music by Arthur Sullivan

DON ALHAMBRA:

stole the Prince and I brought him here And left him gai - ly
ow - ing, I'm much dis - posed to fear, To his ter - ri - ble taste for
sped, and when at the end of a year, I sought that in - fant
chil - dren fol - low'd his old ca - reer (This state - ment can't be

288

pratt - ling | With a high - ly re - spec - ta - ble gon - do - lier, | Who
tip - pling, | That high - ly re - spec - ta - ble gon - do - lier, | Could
cher - ished, | That high - ly re - spec - ta - ble gon - do - lier, | Was
par - ried) | Of a high - ly re - spec - ta - ble gon - do - lier, | Well,

prom - ised the Roy - al babe to rear, | And teach him the trade of a
nev - er de - clare with a mind sin - cere | Which of the two was his
ly - ing a corpse on his hum - ble bier— | I dropp'd a Grand In -
one of the two (who will soon be here) | But which of the two is

ti - mo - neer With his own be - lov - ed brat - ling.
off - spring dear, And which the Roy - al strip - ling!
qui - si - tor's tear That gon - do - lier had per - ished. | A
not quite clear is the Roy - al Prince you mar - ried! | Search

Both of the babes were strong _ and stout, And con - sid - er - ring all things,
Which was which he could nev - er make out, De - spite his best en -
taste for drink, com - bined _ with gout Had dou - bled him up for
in and out and round _ a - bout And you'll dis - cov - er

clev - er. Of *that* there is no man - ner of doubt No
deav - our. Of *that* there is no man - ner of doubt No
ev - er. Of *that* there is no man - ner of doubt No
nev - er. A tale so free from ev - er - y doubt All

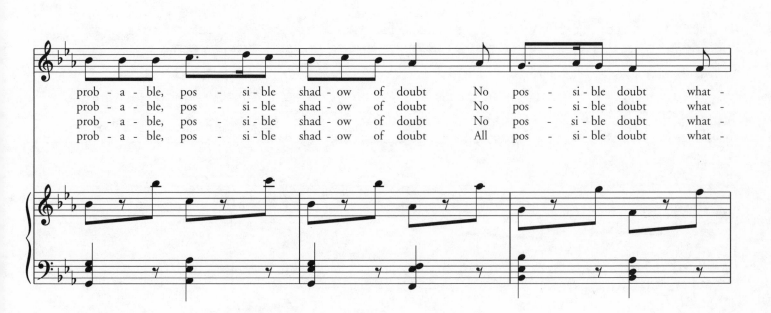

prob - a - ble, pos - si - ble shad - ow of doubt No pos - si - ble doubt what -
prob - a - ble, pos - si - ble shad - ow of doubt No pos - si - ble doubt what -
prob - a - ble, pos - si - ble shad - ow of doubt No pos - si - ble doubt what -
prob - a - ble, pos - si - ble shad - ow of doubt All pos - si - ble doubt what -

When a Merry Maiden Marries

THE GONDOLIERS

Words by W.S. Gilbert
Music by Arthur Sullivan

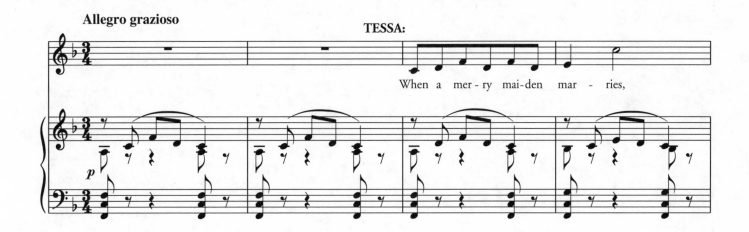

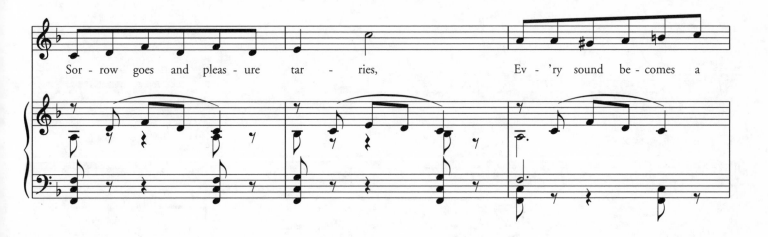

things of yes - ter - day! When you mar - ry mer - ry maid - en,

rall. *a tempo, sostenuto*

Then the air with joy is lad - en; All the cor - ners of the earth Ring with

a tempo

mu - sic sweet - ly played, Wor - ry is mel - o - dious mirth, Grief is

joy in mas - que - rade; Sul - len night is laugh-ing day

Rising Early in the Morning

THE GONDOLIERS

Words by W.S. Gilbert
Music by Arthur Sullivan

* lower notes are for the second verse

duties are de-light-ful, and the priv-i-leg-es great; But the
pleas-ures there are man-y and of wor-ries there are none; And the

priv-i-lege and pleas-ure That we treas-ure be-yond meas-ure Is to
cul-mi-nat-ing pleas-ure That we treas-ure be-yond meas-ure Is the

CHORUS:

run on lit-tle er-rands for the Min-is-ters of State. Oh, _____ phi-
grat-i-fy-ing feel-ing that our du-ty has been done! Oh, _____ phi-

los-o-phers may sing Of the trou-bles of a King; Yet the
los-o-phers may sing Of the trou-bles of a King; But of

duties are de-light-ful, and the priv-i-leg-es great; But the
pleas-ures there are man-y, and of wor-ries there are none; And the

priv-i-lege and pleas-ure That we treas-ure be-yond meas-ure Is to
cul-mi-nat-ing pleas-ure That we treas-ure be-yond meas-ure Is the

run on lit-tle er-rands for the Min-is-ters of State. Af-ter
grat-i-fy-ing feel-ing that our

GIUSEPPE:

rit.   *a tempo*

du-ty has been done!

rit.   *a tempo*

Take a Pair of Sparkling Eyes

THE GONDOLIERS

Words by W.S. Gilbert
Music by Arthur Sullivan

prise, _____ Hav-ing passed the Ru - bi - con. _____ Take a pair of ros - y
spot _____ With the trea - sures rich and rare _____ I've en - deav - oured to __ de -

lips. _____ Take a fig - ure trim - ly planned, __ Such as
fine. _____ Live to love and love to live— __ You will

ad - mi - ra - tion whets __ (Be par - tic - u - lar in this); Take a
ri - pen at your ease, __ Grow-ing on the sun - ny side— Fate has

ten - der lit - tle hand, __ Fringed with dain - ty fin - ger - ettes, __ Press _____
noth - ing more to give. __ You're a dain - ty man to please __ if _____

There Lived a King

THE GONDOLIERS

Words by W.S. Gilbert
Music by Arthur Sullivan

tem - per tri - umphed in ___ his ___ face, And in his heart he found ___ a ___ place For

all the err - ing hu - man race And ev - 'ry ___ wretch - ed fel - low. When ___

he had Rhen - ish wine to drink, It made him ve - ry sad to think That

MARCO & GIUSEPPE:

some, at ___ junk - et or at jink, Must be con - tent with tod - dy, with

So to the top of ev-'ry tree Pro - mo - ted ev - 'ry - bo - dy! Lord

Chan - cel - lors were cheap as sprats, And Bish - ops in their sho - vel hats Were

plen - ti - ful as tab - by cats!— In point of fact, too many. Am -

bas - sa - dors cropped up like hay, Prime Min - is - ters and such as they Grew

King, al - though no one de - nies His heart _ was _ of ab - nor - mal size, Yet

he'd have act - ed oth - er - wise If he had been _ a - cu - ter. The

end is eas - i - ly __ fore - told, When ev - 'ry bless - ed thing _ you _ hold Is

made of sil - ver or of gold, You long for __ sim - ple pew - ter. When __

On the Day When I Was Wedded

THE GONDOLIERS

Words by W.S. Gilbert
Music by Arthur Sullivan

Allegro con fuoco

DUCHESS:

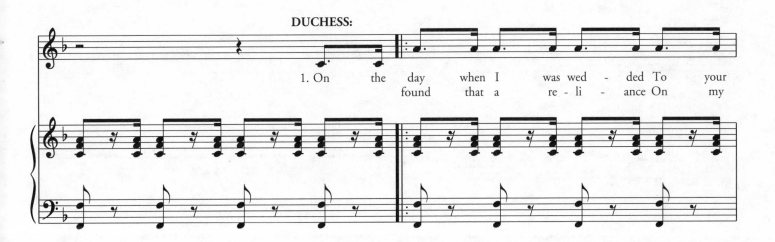

1. On the day when I was wed - ded To your
found that a re - li - ance On my

ad - mi - ra - ble sire, I ac - know - ledge that I dread - ed An ex -
threat - en - ing ap - pear - ance, And a res - o - lute de - fi - ance Of mar -

how   I tried   to tame   your great   pro - gen   -   i - tor—
tamed   your in - sig - nif   -   i - cant   pro - gen   -   i - tor—

at   first!
at

2. But   I

last!

In Ev'ry Mental Lore

UTOPIA LIMITED

Words by W.S. Gilbert
Music by Arthur Sullivan

out   the least   for - mal - i - ty!
keeps   him - self   re -

SCA: SCA:

2. We   spec - ta - ble.   Of a

PHAN: SCA: PHAN:

ty - rant po - lite   He's a   par - a - gon quite.   He's as   mod - est and mild   In his

So Ends My Dream

THE GRAND DUKE

Words by W.S. Gilbert
Music by Arthur Sullivan

Andante con molto espressione

air! ___ All _ is dark - some— All _ is

drea - ry— Bro - ken ev - 'ry pro - mise plight - ed— Sad _ and

sor - ry— weak _ and wea - ry, Ev - 'ry new - born hope _ is

blight - ed! Death _ the Friend or Death _ the Foe, Shall _ I